Ulysses. A Tragedy by Nicholas Rowe

And Performed at the Theatre-Royal in Drury-Lane.

Nicholas Rowe was born in Little Barford, Bedfordshire, England, on June 20th, 1674.

He was educated at Highgate School, and then at Westminster School under the tutelage of Dr. Busby.

In 1688, Rowe became a King's Scholar, and then in 1691 gained entrance into Middle Temple. This was his father's decision (he was a barrister) who felt that his son had made sufficient progress to study law. While at Middle Temple, he decided that studying law was easier if seen as a system of rational government and impartial justice and not as a series of precedents, or collection of positive precepts.

On his father's death, when he was nineteen, he became the master of a large estate and an independent fortune. His future path now was to ignore law and write poetry with a view to eventually writing plays.

The Ambitious Stepmother, Rowe's first play, produced in 1700 at Lincoln's Inn Fields by Thomas Betterton and set in Persepolis, was well received.

This was followed in 1701 by Tamerlane. In this play the conqueror Timur represented William III, and Louis XIV is denounced as Bajazet. It was for many years regularly acted on the anniversary of William's landing at Torbay.

The Fair Penitent (1703), an adaptation of Massinger and Field's The Fatal Dowry, was pronounced by Dr Johnson as one of the most pleasing tragedies ever written in English. He noted that, "The story is domestic, and therefore easily received by the imagination, and assimilated to common life; the diction is exquisitely harmonious, and soft or spritely as occasion requires."

In 1704, he tried his hand at comedy, with The Biter at Lincoln's Inn Fields. The play is said to have amused no one except the author, and Rowe returned to tragedy in Ulysses (1706). For Johnson, this play was to share the fate of many such plays based on mythological heroes, as, "We have been too early acquainted with the poetical heroes to expect any pleasure from their revival"

The Royal Convert (1707) dealt with the persecutions endured by Aribert, son of Hengist and the Christian maiden Ethelinda. The story was set in England in an obscure and barbarous age. Rodogune was a tragic character, of high spirit and violent passions, yet with a wicked with a soul that would have been heroic if it had been virtuous.

Rowe is however well known for his work on Shakespeare's plays. He published the first 18th century edition of Shakespeare in six volumes in 1709. His practical knowledge of the stage helped him divide the plays into scenes and acts, with entrances and exits of the players noted. The spelling of names was normalized and each play prefixed with a dramatis personae. This 1709 edition was also the first to be illustrated, a frontispiece engraving being provided for each play. Unfortunately, Rowe based his text on the discredited Fourth Folio, a failing which many succeeding him also followed.

Rowe also wrote a short biography of William Shakespeare, entitled, Some Account of the Life of Mr. William Shakespear.

For two years (1709-11) he acted as under-secretary to the Duke of Queensberry when he was principal secretary of state for Scotland.

In Dublin in 1712 a revival of his earlier play, Tamerlane, at a time when political passions were running high, the performance provoked a serious riot.

The Tragedy of Jane Shore, played at Drury Lane with Mrs Oldfield in the title role in 1714. It ran for nineteen nights, and kept the stage longer than any other of Rowe's works. In the play, which consists chiefly of domestic scenes and private distress, the wife is forgiven because she repents, and the husband is honoured because he forgives.

The Tragedy of Lady Jane Grey followed in 1715, and as this play was not successful, it was his last foray into the medium.

Whilst his plays met with little success at the time his poems were received extremely well. Although he was not prolific nor his output large the quality was high.

With the accession to the throne of George I he was made a surveyor of customs, and then, in 1715, he succeeded Nahum Tate as poet laureate. It was the high point of his artistic life.

He was also appointed clerk of the council to the Prince of Wales, and in 1718 was nominated by Lord Chancellor Parker as clerk of the presentations in Chancery.

Nicholas Rowe died on December 6th, 1718, and was buried in Westminster Abbey.

Rowe married first a daughter of a Mr Parsons and left a son John. By his second wife Anne, née Devenish, he had a daughter Charlotte.

Index of Contents

DRAMATIS PERSONÆ
MEN
Ulysses, king of Ithaca, concealed for some time under the name of Æthon.
Eurymachus, King of Samos.
Polydamas,   }
Thoon   }   Neighbouring Princes,

Agenor   }   pretenders to the Queen.
Ephialtes   }
Telemachus, son to Ulysses and Penelope.
Antinous, a Nobleman of Ithaca, secretly in love with the Queen.
Cleon   } Friends to Antinous.
Arcas   }
Mentor, tutor to Telemachus.
Eumæus, an old servant, and faithful to Ulysses.
Ceraunus, a Samian officer belonging to Eurymachus.
WOMEN
Penelope, Queen of Ithaca,
Semanthe, Daughter to Eurymachus.

Several Samian and Ithacan Officers and Soldiers, with other Attendants, Men and Women.

SCENE: ITHACA

PROLOGUE

To-night, in honour of the marry'd life,
Our author treats you with a virtuous wife;
A lady, who, for twenty years, withstood
The pressing instances of flesh and blood;
Her husband, still a man of sense reputed,
(Unless this tale his wisdom have confuted,)
Left her at ripe eighteen, to seek renown,
And battle for a harlot at Troy town;
To fill his place, fresh lovers came in shoals,
Much such as now-a-days are Cupid's tools,
Some men of wit, but the most part were fools.
They sent her billets-doux, and presents many,
Of ancient tea and Thericlean china;
Rail'd at the gods, toasted her o'er and o'er,
Dress'd at her, danc'd and fought, and sigh'd, and swore;
In short, did all that man could do to have her,
And damn'd themselves to get into her favour;
But all in vain, the virtuous dame stood buff,
And let them know that she was coxcomb proof:
Messieurs the beaux, what think you of the matter?
Don't you believe old Homer given to flatter?
When you approach, and pressing the soft hand,
Favours, with well-bred impudence, demand,
Is it in woman's weakness to withstand?
Cease to be vain, and give the sex their due;
Our English wives shall prove this story true:
We have our chaste Penelope's, who mourn

Their widow'd beds, and wait their lord's return;
We have our heroes too, who bravely bear,
Far from their home, the dangers of the war;
Who careless of the winter season's rage,
New toils explore, and in new cares engage;
From realm to realm their chief unweary'd goes,
And restless journies on, to give the world repose.
Such are the constant labours of the sun,
Whose active, glorious course is never done;
And though, when hence he parts, with us 'tis night,
Still he goes on, and lends to other worlds his light.
Ye beauteous nymphs, with open arms prepare
To meet the warriors, and reward their care;
May you for ever kind and faithful prove,
And pay their days of toil with nights of love.

ULYSSES

ACT I

SCENE I. A Palace

Enter **TELEMACHUS** and **MENTOR**.

TELEMACHUS
Oh, Mentor! urge no more my royal birth,
Urge not the honours of my race divine,
Call not to my remembrance what I am,
Born of Ulysses, and deriv'd from Jove;
For 'tis the curse of mighty minds oppress'd,
To think what their state is, and what it should be;
Impatient of their lot, they reason fiercely,
And call the laws of Providence unequal.

MENTOR
And therefore wert thou bred to virtuous knowledge,
And wisdom early planted in thy soul;
That thou might'st know to rule thy fiery passions,
To bind their rage, and stay their headlong course,
To bear with accidents, and ev'ry change
Of various life, to struggle with adversity,
To wait the leisure of the righteous gods,
Till they, in their own good appointed hour,
Shall bid thy better days come forth at once,
A long and shining train; till thou, well-pleas'd,
Shalt bow, and bless thy fate, and own the gods are just.

TELEMACHUS
Thou prudent guide and father of my youth,
Forgive my transports, if I seem to lose
The rev'rence to thy sacred precepts due:
'Tis a just rage, and honest indignation.
Ten years ran round e'er Troy was doom'd to fall;
Ten tedious summers, and ten winters more,
By turns have chang'd the seasons since it fell;
And yet we mourn my godlike father's absence,
As if the Grecian arms had ne'er prevail'd,
But Jove and Hector still maintain'd the war.

MENTOR
Tho' absent, yet if oracles are true,
He lives, and shall return. Where'er he wanders,
Pursu'd by hostile Trojan gods, in peril
Of the waste desart, or the foamy deep,
Or nations wild as both, yet courage, wisdom,
And Pallas, guardian of his arms, is with him.

TELEMACHUS
And, Oh, to what does the god's care reserve him?
Where is the triumph shall go forth to meet him?
What Pæan shall be sung to bless his labours?
What voice of joy shall cry, Hail King of Ithaca?
Riot, and wrong, and woful desolation,
Spread o'er the wretched land, shall blast his eyes,
And make him curse the day of his return.

MENTOR
Your guest, the stranger, Æthon.

[Enter **ÆTHON**.

TELEMACHUS
By my life,
And by the great Ulysses, truly welcome.
Oh, thou most worthy Æthon! thou that wert,
In youth, companion of my father's arms,
And partner of his heart, does it not grieve thee,
To see the honour of his royal name
Despis'd and set at nought, his state o'er-run,
Devour'd and parcell'd out by slaves so vile,
That if oppos'd to him, 'twould make comparison
Absurd and monstrous seem, as if to mate
A mole-hill with Olympus?

ÆTHON
He was my friend;
I think I knew him; and, to do him right,
He was a man indeed. Not as these are,
A rioter, or doer of foul wrongs;
But boldly just, and more like what man should be.

TELEMACHUS
From morn till noon, from noon till the shades darken
From evening till the morning dawns again,
Lewdness, confusion, insolence, and uproar,
Are all the bus'ness of their guilty hours;
The cries of maids enforc'd, the roar of drunkards,
Mix'd with the braying of the minstrels' noise,
Who ministers to mirth, ring thro' the palace,
And echo to the arch of heav'n their crimes.
Behold, ye gods, who judge betwixt your creatures,
Behold the rivals of the great Ulysses!

MENTOR
Doubt not but all their crimes, and all thy wrongs
Are judg'd by Nemesis and equal Jove.
Suffer the fools to laugh and loll secure;
This is their day; but there is one behind
For vengeance and Ulysses.

ÆTHON
Till that day,
That day of recompence and righteous justice,
Learn thou, my son, the cruel arts of courts;
Learn to dissemble wrongs, to smile at injuries,
And suffer crimes thou want'st the power to punish;
Be easy, affable, familiar, friendly,
Search, and know all mankind's mysterious ways;
But trust the secret of thy soul to none.
Believe me, seventy years, and all the sorrows
That seventy years bring with them, thus have taught me,
Thus only, to be safe in such a world as this is.

[Enter **ANTINOUS**.

ANTINOUS
Hail to thee, Prince! thou son of great Ulysses,
Offspring of gods, most worthy of thy race;
May ev'ry day like this be happy to thee,
Fruition and success attend thy wishes,
And everlasting glory crown thy youth.

TELEMACHUS

Thou greet'st me like a friend. Come near, Antinous;
May I believe that omen of my happiness,
That joy which dances in thy cheerful eyes?
Or dost thou, for thou know'st my fond, fond heart,
Dost thou betray me to deceitful hopes,
And sooth me, like an infant, with a tale
Of some felicity, some dear delight,
Which thou didst never purpose to bestow?

ANTINOUS

By Cytherea's altar, and her doves,
By all the gentle fires that burn before her,
I have the kindest sounds to bless your ear with,
Nay, and the truest too, I'll swear, I think,
That ever love and innocence inspir'd.

TELEMACHUS

Ha! from Semanthe?

ANTINOUS

From the fair Semanthe,
The gentle, the forgiving—

TELEMACHUS

Soft, my Antinous,
Keep the dear secret safe; wisdom and age
Reason perversely when they judge of love.
A bus'ness of a moment calls me hence, [To **MENTOR**]
That ended, I'll attend the Queen; till then,
Mentor, the noble stranger is thy care—
Fly with me to some safe, some sacred privacy,[To **ANTINOUS**]
There charm my senses with Semanthe's accents,
There pour thy balm into my love-sick soul,
And heal my cares for ever.

[Exeunt **TELEMACHUS** and **ANTINOUS**.

ÆTHON

This smooth speaker,
This supple courtier, is in favour with you.
Mark'd you the Prince, how at this man's approach
The fierceness, rage, and pride of youth declin'd,
His changing visage wore a form more gentle,
And ev'ry feature took a softer turn;
As if his soul, bent on some new employment,
Of different purpose from the thought before,
Had summon'd other counsels, other passions,

And dress'd her in a gay, fantastic garb,
Fit for th' adventure which she meant to prove?
By Jove, I lik'd it not—

MENTOR
The Prince, whose temper
Is open as the day, and unsuspecting,
Esteems him as devoted to his service,
Wise, brave, and just; and since his late return
From Nestor's court at Pyle, he still has held him
In more especial nearness to his heart.

ÆTHON
'Tis rash, and savours of unwary youth.
Tell him, he trusts too far. If I mistook not,
You said he was a wooer.

MENTOR
True, he was;
Noble by birth, and mighty in his wealth,
Proud of the patriot's name and people's praise,
By gifts, by friendly offices, and eloquence,
He won the herd of Ithacans to think him
Ev'n worthy to supply his master's place.

ÆTHON
Unthinking, changeable, ungrateful Ithaca!
But, Mentor, say, the Queen, could she forget
The difference 'twixt Ulysses and his slave?
Did not her soul resent the violation,
And, spite of all the wrongs she labour'd under,
Dash his ambition and presumptuous love?

MENTOR
Still great and royal in the worst of fortunes,
With native power and majesty array'd,
She aw'd this rash Ixion with her frown,
Taught him to bend his abject head to earth,
And own his humbler lot. He stood rebuk'd,
And full of guilty sorrow for the past,
Vow'd to repeat the daring crime no more,
But with humility and loyal service
To purge his fame, and wash the stains away.

ÆTHON
Deceit and artifice! the turn's too sudden;
Habitual evils seldom change so soon,
But many days must pass, and many sorrows,

Conscious remorse and anguish must be felt,
To curb desire, to break the stubborn will,
And work a second nature in the soul,
Ere Virtue can resume the place she lost;
'Tis else dissimulation. But no more;
The ruffling train of suitors are at hand,
Those mighty candidates for love and empire!
'Tis well the gods are mild, when those dare hope
To merit their best gifts by riot and injustice.

[Enter **POLYDAMAS**, **AGENOR**, **THOON**, **EPHIALTES**, and **ATTENDANTS**.

POLYDAMAS
Our souls are out of tune, we languish all,
Nor does the sweet returning of the dawn
Cheer with its usual mirth our drousy spirits,
That droop'd beneath the lazy leaden night.

AGENOR
Can we, who swear we love, smile or be gay,
When our fair queen, the goddess of our vows,
She that adorns our mirth, and gilds our day,
Withholds the beams that only can revive us?

THOON
Night must involve the world till she appear,
The flowers in painted meadows hang their heads,
The birds awake not to their morning songs,
Nor early hinds renew their constant labour;
Ev'n nature seems to slumber till her call,
Regardless of th' approach of any other day.

EPHIALTES
Why is she then withheld, this public good?
Why does she give those hours that should rejoice us,
To tears, perverseness, and to sullen privacy,
While vainly here we waste our lusty youth,
In expectation of the uncertain blessing?

POLYDAMAS
For twice two years this coy, this cruel beauty
Has mock'd our hopes, and cross'd them with delays;
At length the female artifice is plain,
The riddle of her mystic web is known,
Which ere her second choice she swore to weave;
While still the secret malice of the night
Undid the labours of the former day.

AGENOR

Hard are the laws of love's despotic rule,
And ev'ry joy is trebly bought with pain;
Crown we the goblet then, and call on Bacchus,
Bacchus, the jolly god of laughing pleasures,
Bid ev'ry voice of harmony awake,
Apollo's lyre, and Hermes' tuneful shell;
Let wine and music join to swell the triumph,
To sooth uneasy thought, and lull desire.

ÆTHON

Is this the rev'rence due to sacred beauty,
Or these the rights the Cyprian goddess claims?
These rude licentious orgies are for Satyrs,
And such the drunken homage which they pay
To old Silenus nodding on his ass.
But be it as it may, it speaks you well.

EPHIALTES

What says the slave?

THOON

Oh, 'tis the snarler, Æthon!
A privileg'd talker. Give him leave to rail;
Or send for Irus forth, his fellow droll,
And let them play a match of mirth before us,
And laughter be the prize to crown the victor.

ÆTHON

And dost thou answer to reproof with laughter?
But do so still, and be what thou wert born;
Stick to thy native sense, and scorn instruction.
Oh, Folly! what an empire hast thou here!
What temples shall be rais'd to thee! what crowds,
Of slav'ring, hooting, senseless, shameful ideots
Shall worship at thy ignominious altars,
While princes are thy priests!

POLYDAMAS

Why shouldst thou think,
O'erweening, insolent, unmanner'd slave,
That wisdom does forsake the wealth, the honours,
And full prosperity of princes' courts,
To dwell with rags and wretchedness like thine?
Why dost thou call him fool?

ÆTHON

Speech is most free;

It is Jove's gift to all mankind in common.
Why dost thou call me poor, and think me wretched?

POLYDAMAS
Because thou art so.

ÆTHON
Answer to thyself,
And let it serve for thee, and for thy friend.

AGENOR
He talks like oracles, obscure and short.

ÆTHON
I would be understood; but apprehension
Is not thy talent—Midnight surfeits, wine,
And painful undigested morning fumes,
Have marr'd thy understanding.

EPHIALTES
Hence, thou miscreant!
My Lords, this railer is not to be borne.

ÆTHON
And wherefore art thou borne, thou public grievance,
Thou tyrant, born to be a nation's punishment;
To scourge thy guilty subjects for their crimes,
And prove Heaven's sharpest vengeance?

EPHIALTES
Spurn him hence,
And tear the rude unhallow'd railer's tongue
Forth from his throat.

ÆTHON
If brutal violence,
And lust of foul revenge, should urge thee on,
Spite of the Queen and hospitable Jove,
T' oppress a stranger, single, and unarm'd,
Yet, mark me well, I was not born thy vassal;
And wert thou ten times greater than thou art,
And ten times more a king, thus would I meet thee,
Thus naked as I am, I would oppose thee,
And fight a woman's battle with my hands,
Ere thou shouldst do me wrong, and go unpunish'd.

EPHIALTES
Ha! dost thou brave me, dog?

[Coming up to **ÆTHON**.

THOON
Avaunt!

POLYDAMAS
Begone!

[Enter **EURYMACHUS**.

EURYMACHUS
What daughter of old Chaos and the Night,
What fury loiters yet behind the shades,
To vex the peaceful morn with rage and uproar?
Each frowning visage doubly dy'd with wrath,
Your voices in tumultuous clamours rais'd,
Venting reproach, and stirring strong contention.
Say, have you been at variance?—Speak, ye Princes,
Whence grew th' occasion?

ÆTHON
King of Samos, hear me.
To thee, as to a king, worthy the name,
The majesty and right divine of pow'r,
Boldly I dare appeal. This King of Seriphos,

[Pointing to **EPHIALTES**.

This island lord, this monarch of a rock,
He, and his fellow-princes there, yon band
Of eating, drinking lovers, have in scorn
Of the gods' laws, and strangers' sacred privilege,
Offer'd me foul offence, and most unmanly injuries.

EURYMACHUS
Away! It is too much—You wrong your honours,
[To the **WOOERS**.
And stain the lustre of your royal names,
To brawl and wrangle with a thing beneath you.
Are we not chief on earth, and plac'd aloft?
And when we poorly stoop to mean revenge,
We stand debas'd, and level with the slave
Who fondly dares us with his vain defiance.

EPHIALTES
Henceforward let the ribald railer learn
To curb the lawless licence of his speech;

Let him be dumb; we wo' not brook his prating.

EURYMACHUS
Go to! you are too bitter. But no more. [To **ÆTHON**.
Let ev'ry jarring sound of discord cease,
Tune all your thoughts and words to beauty's praise,
To beauty, that, with sweet and pleasant influence,
Breaks like the day-star from the chearful east;
For see, where, circled with a crowd of fair-ones,
Fresh as the spring, and fragrant as its flowers,
Your queen appears, your goddess, your Penelope.

[Enter the **QUEEN**, with **LADIES**, and other **ATTENDANTS**.

Diana thus on Cynthus' shady top,
Or by Eurota's stream, leads to the chase
Her virgin train, a thousand lovely nymphs,
Of form celestial all, troop by her side;
Amidst a thousand nymphs the goddess stands confess'd,
In beauty, majesty, and port divine,
Supreme and eminent.

QUEEN
If these sweet sounds,
This humble fawning phrase, this faithless flattery,
If these known arts could heal my wounded soul,
Could recompense the sorrows of my days,
Or sooth the sighings of my lonely nights,
Well might you hope to wooe me to your wishes,
And win my heart with your fond tales of love.
But since whate'er I've suffer'd for my lord,
From Troy, the winds and seas, the gods, and you,
Is deeply writ within my sad remembrance,
Know, Princes, all your eloquence is vain.

AGENOR
If those bright eyes, that waste their lights with weeping,
Would kindly shine upon Agenor's hopes,
Behold he offers to his charming Queen
His crown, his life, his ever-faithful vows,
What joys soe'er or love or empire yield,
To bless her future days, and make 'em happy all.

POLYDAMAS
Accept my crown, and reign with me in Delos.

THOON
Mine, and the homage of my people wait you.

EPHIALTES

I cannot court you with a silken tale,
With easy ambling speeches, fram'd on purpose,
Made to be spoke in tune—But be my queen,
And leave my plain-spoke love to prove its merit.

QUEEN

And am I yet to learn your love, your faith?
Are not my wrongs gone up to heav'n against you?
Do they not stand before the throne of Jove,
And call incessant on his tardy vengeance?
What sun has shone that has not seen your insolence,
Your wasteful riot, and your impious mirth,
Your scorn of old Laertes' feeble age,
Of my son's youth, and of my woman's weakness?
Ev'n in my palace here, my latest refuge,
(For you are lords of all beside in Ithaca)
With ruffian violence and murd'rous rage,
You menace the defenceless and the stranger,
And from th' unhospitable dwelling drive
Safety and friendly peace.

ÆTHON

For me it matters not;
Wrong is the portion still of feeble age.
My toilsome length of days full oft has taught me
What 'tis to struggle with the proud and powerful:
But 'tis for thy unhappy fate, fair Queen,
'Tis to behold thy beauty and thy virtue,
Transcendant both, worthy the gods who gave them,
And worthy of their care, to see them left,
Abandon'd and forsaken, to rude outrage,
And made a prize for drunkards; 'tis for this
My soul takes fire within, and vainly urges
My cold enervate hand to assert thy cause.

QUEEN

Alas! they scorn the weakness of thy age,
As of my sex—But mark me well, ye Princes!
Whoe'er amongst you dares to lift his hand
Against the hoary head of this old man,
This good old man, this friend of my Ulysses,
Him will I hold my worst, my deadliest foe,
Him shall my curses and revenge pursue,
And mark him from the rest with most distinguish'd hatred.

EPHIALTES

That you are weak, defenceless, and oppress'd,
Impute not to the gods, they have befriended you,
With lavish hands they spread their gifts before you;
What pride, revenge, what wanton love of change,
Or woman's wish can ask, behold, we offer you.
Curse the perverseness of your stubborn will then,
That has delay'd your choice, and in that choice your happiness.

QUEEN
And must I hear this still, and still endure it?
Oh, rage! dishonour! wretched, helpless Queen!
Return, return, my hero, my Ulysses;
Bring him again, you cruel seas and winds;
Troy and adult'rous Paris are no more;
Restore him then, you righteous gods of Greece,
T' avenge himself and me upon these tyrants,
And do a second justice here at home.

EURYMACHUS
Amongst the mighty manes of the Greeks,
Great names, and fam'd for highest deeds in war,
His honour'd shade rests from the toils of life,
In everlasting indolence and ease,
Careless of all your pray'rs and vain complainings,
Which the winds bear away, and scatter in their wantonness.
Turn those bright eyes then from despair and death,
And fix your better hopes among the living;
Fix them on one who dares, who can defend you,
One worthy of your choice.

QUEEN
If my free soul
Must stoop to this unequal hard condition,
If I must make this second hated choice,
Yet by connubial Juno, here I swear,
None shall succeed my lord, but that brave man
That dares avenge me well upon the rest.
Then let whoever dares to love be bold,
Be, like my former hero, made for war,
Able to bend the bow, and toss the spear;
For ev'ry wrong his injur'd Queen has found,
Let him revenge and pay it with a wound;
Fierce from the slaughter let the victor come,
And tell me that my foes have met their doom;
Then plight his faith upon his bloody sword,
And be, what my Ulysses was, my best, my dearest lord.

[Exeunt all but ÆTHON.

ÆTHON

Oh, matchless proof of faith and love unchang'd!
Left in the pride, the wishing warmth of youth,
For ten long years, and ten long years to that,
And yet so true! Beset with strong allurements,
With youth, proud pomp, and soft bewitching pleasure,
'Tis wonderful! and wives in later times
Shall think it all the forgery of wit,
A fable curiously contriv'd t' upbraid
Their fickle easy faith and mock them for their lightness.
But see, the Samian King returns.

[Enter **EURYMACHUS**.

EURYMACHUS

I sought you
Amidst the crowd of princes who attend
The Queen to Juno's temple.

ÆTHON

When I worship,
And bow myself before the awful gods,
I mingle not with those who scorn their laws,
With raging, brutal, loose, voluptuous crowds,
Who take the gods for gluttons like themselves.

EURYMACHUS

This sullen garb, this moody discontent,
Sits on thee well, and I applaud thy anger,
Thy just disdain of this licentious rout:
Yet all are not like these; nor ought thy quarrel
Be carry'd on to all mankind in common.

ÆTHON

Perhaps the untaught plainness of my words
May make you think my manners rude and savage;
But know, my country is the land of liberty;
Phæacia's happy isle, that gave me birth,
Forbids not any to speak plain and truly;
Sincere and open are we, roughly honest,
Upright in deed, tho' simple in our speech,
As meaning not to flatter or offend;
The use of words we have, but not the art;
And ev'n as nature dictates, so we speak.

EURYMACHUS

Now, by great Juno, guardian of our Samos,

In strong description hast thou well express'd
That manly virtue I would make a friend of.
Nor thou, brave Æthon, shalt disdain our amity,
Our proffer'd love; for know, that kings, like gods,
With all things good adorn their own creation,
And where their favour fixes, there is happiness.

ÆTHON

Yes, Sir, you are a king, a great one too;
My humble birth has cast me far beneath you,
And made me for the proffer'd grace unfit;
Friendship delights in equal fellowship,
Where parity of rank and mutual offices
Engage both sides alike, and keep the balance even.
'Tis irksome to a gen'rous, grateful soul,
To be oppress'd beneath a load of favours,
Still to receive, and run in debt to friendship,
Without the pow'r of paying something back.

EURYMACHUS

I know thee grateful; just and gen'rous minds
Are always so; nor is thy pow'r so scanty,
But that it may vie with a king's munificence,
May make me large amends for all my bounty,
May bless me with a benefit I want,
And give me that which my soul most desires:
The Queen—

ÆTHON

How, Sir, the Queen!

EURYMACHUS

The beauteous Queen,
That summer-sun in full meridian glory,
Brighter than the faint promise of the spring,
With blessings ripen'd to the gath'rer's hand,
Mature for joy, and in perfection lovely;
Ev'n she!
The pride of Greece, the wish of youthful princes,
Severe, and cold, and rigid as she is,
Looks gently on thee, Æthon, she beholds thee
With kind regard, and listens to thy counsels.

ÆTHON

Be still, thou beating heart! [Aside.] Well, Sir, go on.

EURYMACHUS

No more, there needs no more; thy piercing wit,

I read it in thy eyes, hath found my purpose.
Be favourable then, be friendly to me;
Nay, I'll conjure thee, by my hopes, by thine,
Whether they follow wealth, or power, or fame,
Or what desires soe'er warm thy old breast,
Counsel me, aid me, teach me, be my friend.

ÆTHON

Suppose me such, what should my friendship profit you?

EURYMACHUS

Oh, by ten thousand ways! Has not that age
That turn'd thy rev'rend locks so silver white,
Has it not giv'n thee skill in woman-kind,
Sagacious wisdom to explore their subtleties,
Their coy aversions, and their eager appetites,
Their false denials, and their secret yieldings?
Yet more, thy friendship with her former lord
Gives thee a right to speak, and be believ'd.

ÆTHON

Then you would have me wooe her for you, win her,
This queen, this wife of him that was my friend?

EURYMACHUS

Thou speak'st me well; of him that was my friend.
His death has broke those bonds of love and friendship,
And left me free and worthy to succeed
Both in her heart and thine.

ÆTHON

Excuse me, Sir,
Nor think I meant to question your high worth.
I am but ill at praising, or my tongue
Had spoke the great things that my heart thinks of you:
Suppose me wholly yours—Yet do you hold
This sov'reign beauty made of such light stuff,
So like the common changelings of her sex,
That he that flatter'd, sigh'd, and spoke her fair,
Could win her from her stubborn resolution,
And chaste reservedness, with his sweet persuasion?

EURYMACHUS

No, were she formed like them, she were a conquest
Beneath a monarch's love, or Æthon's wit.
Not but I think she has her warmer wishes,
'Twere monstrous else, and nature had deny'd
Her choicest blessing to her fairest creature,

Her soft desires, that steal abroad unseen,
Like silver Cynthia sliding from her orb,
At dead of night, to young Endymion's arms.

ÆTHON
How! think you so?—But so 'tis true it may be;
The best of all the sex is but a woman;
And why should Nature break her rule for one,
To make one true, when all the rest are false?
To find those wishes then, those fond desires,
To trace the fulsome haunts of wanton appetite,
She must be try'd.

EURYMACHUS
That to thy care, my Æthon,
Thy wit, and watchful friendship, I commend.

ÆTHON
Yes, Sir, be certain on't, she shall be try'd;
Thro' all the winding mazes of her thoughts,
Thro' all her joys, her sorrows, and her fears,
Thro' all her truth and falshood, I'll pursue her;
She shall be subtler than deceit itself,
And prosperously wicked, if she 'scape me.

EURYMACHUS
Thou art my genius, and my happier hours
Depend upon thy providence and rule.
This day, at her return from Juno's altar,
I have obtain'd an hour of private conference.

ÆTHON
What! private, said you? 'Twas a mark of favour,
Distinguishingly kind.

EURYMACHUS
Somewhat I urg'd
That much concern'd her honour and her safety;
Nay, ev'n the life of her belov'd Telemachus,
Which to her ear alone I would disclose.
Thou shalt be present—How I mean to prove her,
Which way to shake the temper of her soul,
And where thy aid may stand me most in stead,
I will instruct thee as we pass along.

ÆTHON
I wait you, Sir.

EURYMACHUS
Nor doubt of the success.
This stubborn beauty shall be taught compliance.
Fair daughter of the ocean, smiling Venus,
Thou joy of gods and men, assist my purpose!
Thy Cyprus and Cythera leave a while,
Thy Paphian groves and sweet Idalian hill,
To fix thy empire in this rugged isle;
Bring all thy fires from ev'ry lover there,
To warm this coy, this cruel frozen fair;
Let her no more from nature's laws be free,
But learn obedience to thy great decree,
Since gods themselves submit to Fate, and thee.

[Exeunt.

ACT II

Enter **ANTINOUS**, **CLEON**, and **ARCAS**.

ANTINOUS
'Tis thus, my fellow-citizens, and friends,
'Tis thus unhappy Ithaca must groan
Beneath the bondage of a foreign lord;
A needy upstart race of hungry strangers
Shall swarm upon the land, eat its increase,
Devour the labours of the toiling hind,
And gather all the wealth and honours of our isle.

CLEON
The silken minions of the Samian court,
To lord it o'er the province shall be sent,
To rule the state, to be the chiefs in war,
And lead our hardy Ithacans to battle.
Freedom and right shall cease, our corn, wine, oil,
The fatness of the year, shall all be theirs;
Our modest matrons, and our virgin daughters,
Ev'n all we hold most dear, shall be the spoil,
The prey of our imperious haughty masters.

ARCAS
Would I could say I did not fear these evils!

ANTINOUS
Oh, honest Arcas! 'tis too plain a danger.
The Queen, requir'd by public voice to wed,

To end at once the hopes and riotous concourse
Of princely guests, contending for her love,
O'er-passing all the noblest of our isle,
Inclines to fix her choice on proud Eurymachus.

CLEON
Why rides the Samian fleet within our harbour,
But to support their tyrant's title here?
With causes feign'd they linger long, pretending
Rude winter seas, with omens that forbid
The frighted mariner to leave the shore;
While Neptune smooths his waters for their passage,
And gently whistling winds invite their sails,
As if they wish'd to waft them back to Samos.

ARCAS
Ulysses is no more; the partial gods,
Who favour'd Priam and his hapless race,
Have pour'd their wrath on his devoted head,
And now, in some far distant realm, expos'd,
To glut the vulture's and the lion's maw,
Or in the oozy bottom of the deep,
Full many a fathom down, the hero lies,
And never shall return—What then remains,
But that our country fly to thee for succour, [To **ANTINOUS**]
To thee, the noblest of the lords of Ithaca?
And since, so fate ordains, our Queen must wed,
Be thou her second choice, be thou our ruler,
And save our nation from a foreign yoke.

ANTINOUS
You are my friends, and over-rate my worth;
But witness for me, for you still have known me,
Whene'er my country's service calls me on,
No enterprise so doubtful, or so dangerous,
But I will boldly prove it, to preserve thee,
Oh, Ithaca! from bondage.

CLEON
Wherefore urge you not
Your suit among the rest?

ANTINOUS
The cruel Queen
Rejects my humble vows with angry scorn:
And when I once presum'd to speak my passion,
She call'd it insolence—Since then I've strove
To hide th' unlucky folly from all eyes

But yours, my friends, who view my naked soul.

ARCAS
Avow your flame in public, tell the world,
Antinous is worthy of a queen:
So many valiant hands shall own your cause,
So shall the voice in Ithaca be for you,
The Queen shall own your love has made her great,
And giv'n her back an empire she had lost.

ANTINOUS
Think not I dream the hours of life away,
Supine, and negligent of love and glory;
No, Arcas, no; my active mind is busy,
And still has labour'd with a vast design;
Ere long the beauteous birth will be disclos'd,
Then shall your pow'rs come forth, your swords and counsels,
And manifest the love you bear Antinous.
Till then be still—To favour my design,
With low submissions, with obsequious duty,
And vows of friendship fit to flatter boys with,
I've wound myself into the Prince's heart.

CLEON
'Tis said the love-sick youth doats ev'n to death
Upon the Samian Princess, fair Semanthe.

ANTINOUS
Let it go on; 'tis a convenient dotage,
And suits my purpose well—The youth by nature
Is active, fiery, bold, and great of soul;
Love is the bane of all these noble qualities,
The sickly fit that palls ambition's appetite;
And therefore have I nurs'd the fond disease,
Inspiring lazy wishes, sighs, and languishings,
Unactive dreaming sloth, and womanish softness,
To freeze his veins, and quench his manly fires.
The froward God of Love, to boast his pow'r,
Has bred of late some little jars between them;
But 'twas my care to reconcile their follies,
And, if my augury deceives me not,
This day a priest in private makes them one,
Unknown or to the Queen or to Eurymachus.
But see! they come—Retire.

[Enter **TELEMACHUS** and **SEMANTHE**.

Do, sigh, and smile,

And print thy lips upon the soft white hand;
Sceptres and crowns are trifles none regard,
That can be bless'd with such a joy as this is.

[Exeunt **ANTINOUS**, **CLEON** and **ARCAS**.

TELEMACHUS
Yes, my Semanthe, still I will complain,
Still I will murmur at thee, cruel maid,
For all that pain thou gav'st my heart but now.
What god, averse to innocence and love,
Could shake thy gentle soul with such a storm?
Just at that happy moment, when the priest
Had join'd our hands, thou start'dst as death had struck thee,
And, sighing, cry'd, Ah, no!—it is impossible!

SEMANTHE
And yet, Oh, my lov'd lord! yet I am yours;
This hand has giv'n me to you, and this heart,
This heart, that achs with tenderness, confirm'd it.

TELEMACHUS
And yet thou art not mine; else why this sorrow?
Why art thou wet with weeping, as the earth,
When vernal Jove descends in gentle show'rs,
To cause increase, and bless the infant year,
When ev'ry spiry grass, and painted flow'r,
Is hung with pearly drops of heav'nly rain?

SEMANTHE
Ye woods and plains, and all ye virgin dryads,
Happy companions of those woods and plains,
Why was I forc'd to leave your chearful fellowship,
To come and lose my peace of mind at Ithaca?
And, Oh, Semanthe! wherefore didst thou listen
To that dear voice? Why didst thou break thy vow,
Made to the huntress, Cynthia, and her train?
Ah, say, fond maid! say, wherefore didst thou love?

TELEMACHUS
Alas, my gentle love! how have I wrong'd thee?
By what unwilling crime have I offended,
That thus with dreaming eyes thou shouldst complain,
Thus dash my joys, and quench those holy fires,
By yellow Hymen's torch so lately lighted,
Thus stain this blessed day, our bridal day,
With the detested omen of thy sorrows.

SEMANTHE

Of what should I accuse thee? Thou art noble,
Thy heart is soft, is pitiful, and tender;
And thou wilt never wrong the poor Semanthe.
And yet—

TELEMACHUS

What means't thou?

SEMANTHE

What have we been doing?

TELEMACHUS

A deed of happiness.

SEMANTHE

Are we not marry'd?

TELEMACHUS

We are; and like the careful, thrifty hind,
Who, provident of winter, fills his stores
With all the various plenty of the autumn,
We've hoarded up a mighty mass of joy,
To last for all our years that are to come,
And sweeten ev'ry bitter hour of life.

SEMANTHE

Fain would I sooth my soul with these sweet hopes,
Forget the anguish of my waking cares,
And all those boding dreams that haunt my slumbers
Last night, when after many a heavy sigh,
And many a painful thought, the god of sleep,
Insensible and soft, had stole upon me;
Methought I found me by a murm'ring brook,
Reclin'd at ease upon the flow'ry margin,
And thou, thou first and last of all my thoughts,
Thou dear, eternal object of my wishes,
Close by my side wert laid—

TELEMACHUS

Delightful vision!
And, Oh, Oh, pity that it was not real!

SEMANTHE

Awhile on many a pleasing theme we talk'd,
And mingled sweet discourse; when on the sudden,
The cry of hounds, the jolly huntsman's horn,
With all the chearful music of the chase,

Surpris'd my ear, and straight a troop of nymphs,
Once the dear partners of my virgin heart,
Flew lightly by us, eager of the sport;
Last came the goddess, great Latona's daughter,
With more than mortal grace she stood confest,
I saw the golden quiver at her back,
And heard the sounding of her silver bow;
Abash'd I rose, and lowly made obeysance;
But she, not sweet, nor affable, nor smiling,
As once she wont, with stern regard beheld me;
And wherefore dost thou loiter here, she said,
Of me, thy fellows, and our sports unmindful?
Return, thou fugitive; nor vainly hope
To dress thy bridal bed, and waste thy youth
In wanton pleasures, and inglorious love!
A virgin at my altar wert thou vow'd,
'Tis fix'd by fate, and thou art mine for ever.
With that she snatch'd a chaplet from my hand,
Which for thy head in fondness I had wove,
And bore me swiftly with her.—In my flight,
Backwards, methought, I turn'd my eyes to thee,
But found thee not, for thou wert vanish'd from me,
And in thy place my father lay extended
Upon the earth, a bloody lifeless corse;
Struck to the very heart, I shriek'd aloud,
And waking, found my tears upon my pillow.

TELEMACHUS
Vex not thy peaceful soul, my fair Semanthe,
Nor dread the anger of the awful gods,
Safe in thy native unoffending innocence.
Still when the golden sun withdraws his beams,
And drowzy night invades the weary world,
Forth flies the god of dreams, fantastic Morpheus,
Ten thousand mimic phantoms fleet around him,
Subtle as air, and various in their natures,
Each has ten thousand thousand diff'rent forms,
In which they dance confus'd before the sleeper,
While the vain god laughs to behold what pain
Imaginary evils give mankind.

SEMANTHE
Not happy omens that approve our wishes,
When bright with flames the chearful altar shines,
And the good gods are gracious to our offerings,
Not oracles themselves, that speak us happy,
Could charm my fears, and lull my froward sorrows,
Like the dear voice of him whom my soul loves.

Ev'n while thou spok'st my breast begun to glow,
I felt sweet hopes, and joy, and peace returning,
And all the fires of life were kindled up anew.

TELEMACHUS
Hence then, thou meager care, ill-boding melancholy,
Anxious disquiet, and heart-breaking grief,
Fly to your native seats, where deep below
Old night and horror with the furies dwell,
Love and the joyful genial bed disclaim you;
To-night a thousand little laughing Cupids
Shall be our guard, and wakeful watch around us;
No sound, no thought shall enter to disturb us,
But sacred silence reign; unless, sometimes,
We sigh and murmur with excess of happiness.

SEMANTHE
Alas, my Lord!

TELEMACHUS
Again that mournful sound!

SEMANTHE
What other pain is this? What other fear,
So diff'rent quite from what I felt before?
Alternate heat and cold shoot through my veins;
Now a chill dew hangs faintly on my brow,
And now with gentle warmth I glow all o'er;
Short are my sighs, and nimbly beats my heart,
I gaze on thee with joy, and yet I tremble;
'Tis pain and pleasure blended, both at once,
'Tis life and death, or something more than either.

TELEMACHUS
Thus untry'd soldiers, when the trumpet sounds,
Expect the combat with uncertain passions;
Thus Nature speaks in unexperienc'd maids,
And thus they blush, and thus like thee they tremble.
At even, when the queen retires to rest,
I'll meet thee here, and take thee to my arms,
Thy best, thy surest refuge.—
But see! the stranger Æthon comes; retire;
I would not have his watchful eye observe us.

[Enter **ÆTHON**.

I charge thee loiter not, but haste to bless me,
Haste, at th' appointed hour—

Think with what eager hopes, what rage I burn,
For ev'ry tedious minute how I mourn;
Think how I call thee cruel for thy stay,
And break my heart with grief, for thy unkind delay.

[Exeunt **TELEMACHUS** and **SEMANTHE**.

ÆTHON
Ha! what, so close! How cautious to avoid me!
As who should say, old man, you are too wise,
What has my youth to do with your instructions,
While folly is pleasant to my taste,
And damn'd destruction wears a face so fair?
This Samian king is happy in his arts;
His daughter, vow'd a virgin to Diana,
Is brought to play the wanton here at Ithaca:
No matter for religion; let the gods
Look to their rites themselves: the youth grows fond,
Just to their wish! and swears himself their vassal.
His mother follows next—But soft—They come;
Now to put on the pander—That's my office.

[Enter the **QUEEN** and **EURYMACHUS**.

QUEEN
Have I not answer'd oft, it is in vain,
In vain to urge me with this hateful subject?
As thou art noble, pity me, Eurymachus,
Add not new weight of sorrows to my days,
That drag too slow, too heavily along;
Compel me not to curse my life, my being,
To curse each morn, each chearful morn, that dawns
With healing comfort on its balmy wings,
To ev'ry wretched creature but myself;
To me it brings more pain, and iterated woes.

EURYMACHUS
Oh, god of eloquence, bright Maia's son!
Teach me what more than mortal grace of speech,
What sounds can move this fierce relentless fair,
This cruel Queen, that pityless beholds
My heart that bleeds for her, my humble knee,
In abject low submission bent to earth,
To deprecate her scorn, and beg in vain,
One gracious word, one favourable look.

QUEEN
Count back the tedious years, since first my hero

Forsook these faithful arms to war with Troy;
And yet in all that long, long tract of time,
Witness, ye chaster powers, if e'er my thoughts
Have harbour'd any other guest but him;
Remember, king of Samos, what I have been,
Then think if I can change—Æthon, come near.

[ÆTHON comes forward.

Good honest man! how rare is truth like thine!
Thou great example of a loyal friend!

ÆTHON
Oh, lady, spare that praise; if few like me
Are friends, yet none have ever lov'd like you;
Why what a mighty space is twenty years!
'Tis irksome to remembrance, to look back
Upon your youth, that happier part of life,
Like some fair field, of rich and fertile soil,
That might have blest the owner with abundance,
But left unheeded, like a barren moor,
Lies senceless, wild, uncultivate, and waste.

QUEEN
Alas!

EURYMACHUS
Were youth and beauty giv'n in vain?
Why were the gods so lavish of their gifts
To one whose sullen pride neglects to use them,
As if she scorn'd the care heav'n took to make her happy?

ÆTHON
More than enough of sorrow have you known;
Give ease at length to your afflicted soul,
Be comforted, and now while time is yours,
Taste the good things of life, yet e'er they perish,
Yet e'er the happy season pass away.

QUEEN
What sov'reign balm, what heav'nly healing art,
Can cure a heart so torn with grief as mine,
Can stay this never-ceasing stream of tears,
And once more make my senses know delight?

EURYMACHUS
What god can work that miracle but Love?
Love, who dispenses joy to heav'n itself,

And cheats his fellow-gods more than their nectar,
'Till wrapt with vast, unutterable pleasures,
Such as immortal natures only know,
Each owns his pow'r, and blesses the sweet boy.

QUEEN
Now, Æthon, by thy friendship to my Lord,
Answer, I charge thee, to this cruel king;
Demand if it be noble to prophane
My virtue thus, with loose dishonest courtship.

ÆTHON
Are love and virtue then such mortal foes,
That they must never meet?

QUEEN
Never with me,
Unless my Lord return.

ÆTHON
Vain expectation!

QUEEN
Ha! Surely I mistook!—What said'st thou, Æthon?

ÆTHON
That you have waited long for that return,
Wasted too much of life, and cast away
Those precious hours, that might have been employ'd
To better use than weeping.

QUEEN
This from thee!
Oh, faithless! Truth is vanish'd then indeed.
Oh, Æthon!—art thou too become my enemy!

ÆTHON
If, to reward your faith to lost Ulysses,
I pray the gods to heap their blessings on you,
To make you mistress of a mighty nation,
An empire greater, nobler than your own,
And crown you with this valiant monarch's love,
If this be enmity, you may accuse me.

QUEEN
Dost thou solicit for him? Dost thou dare
Invade my peace, my virtue?

ÆTHON
Not for him,
But for the common happiness of both.

QUEEN
Traitor! no more—at length thy wicked arts,
Thy false dissembled friendship for my Lord,
Thy pious journey hither for his sake,
Thy care of me, my son, and of the state,
Thy praise, thy counsels, and thy shew of virtue,
So holy, so adorn'd with rev'rend age,
All are reveal'd, and thou confest a villain;
Hire, and the sordid love of gain have caught thee;
Gold has prevail'd upon thee to betray me,
And bargain for my honour with this prince.

[Pointing to **EURYMACHUS**.

ÆTHON
It grieves me I offend you—sure I am,
I meant it as a friend.

QUEEN
Hence from my sight!

EURYMACHUS
Æthon, no more—Since love and willing friendship
Employ their pious offices in vain,
Learn we, henceforth, from this imperious beauty,
Learn we, from her example, to be cruel;
And though our softer passions rest unsatisfy'd,
Yet the more fierce, the manly, and the rough,
Shall be indulg'd and riot to excess.
Up then, Revenge, and arm thee, thou fell fury,
Up then, and shake thy hundred iron whips;
To-day I vow to sacrifice to thee,
And slake thy horrid thirst with draughts of royal gore.

QUEEN
What says the tyrant? [Aside] Oh, Eurymachus!
What fatal purpose has thy heart conceiv'd?
What means that rage that lightens in thy eyes,
That flashes fierce, and menaces destruction?

EURYMACHUS
The lambent fire of love prevails no more,
And now another mightier flame succeeds;
Vaunt not too soon, nor triumph in thy scorn;

For know, proud Queen, in spite of thy disdain,
There is a way ev'n yet to reach thy heart.
Thou hast a son, the darling of thy eyes—

QUEEN
Oh, fatal thought!
Fear, like the hand of death, hath seiz'd my heart,
Cold, chilling cold—my son! Oh, my Telemachus!

ÆTHON [Aside]
That stroke was home—now, Virtue, hold thy own.

EURYMACHUS
Know then, that son is in my pow'r, and holds
His frail uncertain being at my pleasure;
And when I frown, death and destruction, greedy,
Watchful, intent like tygers on their prey,
Start sudden forth, and seize the helpless boy.
Three hundred chosen warriors from my fleet,
Who undiscern'd, in parties, and by stealth,
Late came a-shore, now wait for my commands;
Think on them as the ministers of fate,
For when I bid them execute, 'tis done.

QUEEN
If, as my soul presages from those terrors
Which gather on thy stern, tempestuous brow,
Thou art severely bent on death and vengeance,
Yet hear me, hear a wretch's only pray'r,
Oh, spare the innocent, spare my Telemachus,
Let not the ruffian's sword nor murd'rous violence
Cut off the noble promise of his youth,
Oh, spare him, and let all thy rage fall here;
Remember, 'twas this haughty, stubborn queen
Refus'd thy love, and let her feel thy hate.

EURYMACHUS
A secret joy glides through my sullen heart,
To see so fair a suitor kneel before me.
But what have I to do with thoughts like these?
Æthon, go bear this ring to bold Ceraunus,
The valiant leader of our Samian band;
My last of orders, which this morn I gave him,
Bid him perform; haste thou, and see it done.

QUEEN
Stay I conjure thee, Æthon—Cruel king!
Speak, answer me, unfold this dreadful secret;

Where points this sudden, dark, mysterious mischief?
Say, at the head of what devoted wretch
This winged thunder aims—Say, while my fears
Have left me yet a little life to hear thee.

EURYMACHUS
Already dost thou dread the gath'ring storm,
That grumbles in the air, preluding ruin?
But mark the stroke, keep all thy tears for that,
Too soon it shall be told thee—Æthon, hence.

QUEEN [Holding **ÆTHON**]
Not for thy life—No, not till thou hast heard me.
[To **EURYMACHUS**]
Too well, alas! I understand my fate.
How have I been, among the happy mothers,
Call'd the most happy, now the most miserable:
Then barren, comfortless sate down and wept,
When they compar'd their marriage-beds with mine;
The fruitful, when they boasted of their numbers,
With envy and unwilling praise, confest
That I had all their blessings in my one.
Our virgins, when they met him, sigh'd and blush'd,
Matrons and wives beheld him as a wonder,
And gazing crouds pursu'd and blest him as he pass'd.
But then, his youth! his tenderness! his piety!
Oh, my Telemachus! my son! my son!

EURYMACHUS
And what are all these tears and helpless wailings,
What poor amends to injur'd love and me?
How have I mourn'd thy scorn, unkind and cruel?
How have I melted in unmanly weeping?
How have I taught the stubborn rocks of Ithaca,
And all the sounding shore to echo my complainings?
And hast thou e'er relented? Now mourn thou,
And murmur not, nor think thy lot too hard,
Since equal justice pays thee but thy own.

QUEEN
Oh, didst thou know what agonies I feel,
Hard as thou art, thou wouldst have pity on me:
Death is too poor a name, for that means rest,
But 'tis despair—'tis mad—tormenting rage,
'Tis terrible—'tis bitter pain—it is
A mother's mourning for her only son.

ÆTHON

Now, now her labouring heart is rent with anguish!
Oh, nature, how affecting are thy sorrows!
How moving, melting in a mother's eyes!
So silver Thetis, on the Phrygian shore,
Wept for her son, fore-knowing of his fate,
The sea-nymphs sate around, and join'd their tears,
While from his lowest deep old father ocean
Was heard to groan, in pity of their pain. [Aside.

EURYMACHUS
Fair mourner, rise—Thus far thou hast prevail'd.

[Offering to raise her.

If, to atone for all I have endur'd,
For all thy cold neglect, thy arts, delays,
For all my years of anxious expectation,
This night thou give thy beauties to my arms;
This night! for love, impatient of my wrongs,
Allows not ev'n a moment's space beyond it;
The prince, thy lov'd Telemachus, shall live,
And danger and distress shall never know thee more.

QUEEN
Oh, shame! Oh, modesty! connubial truth
And spotless purity! Ye heav'nly train!
Have I preserv'd you in my secret soul,
To give you up at last, then plunge in guilt,
Abandon'd to dishonour and pollution!
Oh, never! never! let me first be rack'd,
Torn, scatter'd by the winds, plung'd in the deep,
Or bound amidst the flames—Oh, friendly earth
Open thy bosom—And thou, Proserpine,
Infernal Juno, mighty queen of shades,
Receive me to thy dark, thy dreadful empire,
And hide me, save me from this tyrant's fury.

ÆTHON [Aside]
Oh, racking, racking pain of secret thought!

EURYMACHUS
Hence! hence, thou trifler, love! fond, vain deceiver!
I cast, I tear thee out—Æthon, begone!

QUEEN
Then drag me too!—Yet hear me once, once more,
For I will speak to thee of love!—of rage!
Of death! of madness! and eternal chaos!

EURYMACHUS [To ÆTHON]
Away, thou loiterer!

ÆTHON
Then I must go?

QUEEN
Eurymachus!

[Holding out her hand to him.

EURYMACHUS
Speak—

QUEEN
Mercy!

EURYMACHUS
Love!

QUEEN
Telemachus.

EURYMACHUS
My queen! My goddess! Art thou kind at last!
Oh, softly, softly breathe the charming sound,
And let it gently steal upon my soul,
Gently as falls the balmy dew from heav'n,
Or let thy kind consenting eyes speak for thee,
And bring me the sweet tidings from thy heart;
She yields! Immortal gods, she yields!

QUEEN
Where is he?
Where is my son? Oh, tell me, is he safe,
Swear to me some most sacred solemn oath,
Swear my Telemachus is free from danger.

EURYMACHUS
Hear me, great Jove, father of gods and men,
And thou, blue Neptune, and thou, Stygian Pluto,
Hear, all ye greater and ye lesser powers,
That rule in heav'n, in earth, in seas, and hell,
While to my queen, on this fair hand I swear,
That royal youth, that best-lov'd son is safe,
Nor dies, unless his mother urge his fate.
At night, a priest, by faithful Æthon's care,

In private shall attend at thy apartment,
There while rich gums we burn, and spicy odours,
The gods of marriage and of love invoking,
I will renew my vows, and at thy feet,
Devote ev'n all my pow'rs to thy command.

QUEEN
'Till then be kind, and leave me to myself;
Leave me to vent the fulness of my breast,
Pour out the sorrows of my soul alone,
And sigh myself, if possible, to peace.
Oh, thou dear youth, for whom I feel again
My throes, and twice endure a mother's pain;
Well had I dy'd to save thee, Oh, my son!
Well, to preserve thy life, had giv'n my own;
But when the thoughts of former days return,
When my lost virtue, fame, and peace I mourn,
The joys which still thou gav'st me I forget,
And own I bought thee at a price too great.

[Exit.

EURYMACHUS
At length we have prevail'd: fear, doubt and shame,
Those peevish female virtues, fly before us,
And the disputed field at last is ours.

ÆTHON
Yes, you have conquer'd, have approv'd yourself
A master in the knowledge of the sex.
What then remains, but to prepare for triumph,
To rifle all the spoils of captive beauty,
And reap the sweet reward of your past labours?
What of the prince?

EURYMACHUS
He lives, but must be mine,
And my Semanthe's love the band to hold him;
But to to-morrow's dawn leave we that care:
The present day, for deep, for vast designs,
And hardy execution is decreed.
This night, according to their wonted riot,
The rival princes mean to hold a feast.

ÆTHON
I mark'd but now the mighty preparation,
When to the hall the sweating slaves past in,
Bending beneath the massie goblets' weight,

Whose each capacious womb, fraught with rich juice
Drawn from the Chian and the Lesbian grape,
Portended witless mirth, vain laughter, boasting,
Contentious brawling, madness, mischief, and foul murder;
While to appease the glutton's greedy maw
Whole herds are slain, more than suffice for hecatombs,
Ev'n more than zeal, with pious prodigality,
Bestows upon the gods to feed their priests with.

EURYMACHUS
Then mark me well, or e'er the rowling night
Hath finish'd half her course, the fumy vapours
And mounting spirits of the deep-drunk bowl,
Shall seize the brains of these carousing lovers;
Then shalt thou, Æthon, with my valiant Samians,
Arm'd and appointed all at thy command,
Surround the hall, and on our common foes
At once revenge my queen, thyself, and me.

ÆTHON
Ha! At a blow!—'tis just—'tis greatly thought!
By Jove th' avenger, 'twill be noble slaughter;
Nor doubt the event. I answer for them all,
Ev'n to a man.

EURYMACHUS
Thine then be all the care,
While I with softer pleasures crown my hours,
And revel in delight.

ÆTHON
How! At that hour!

[Starting.

Ha!—In enjoyment! Can that be?

EURYMACHUS
It must.
Fierce for the joy, in secret, and alone
I'll steal upon my love.

ÆTHON
Stay! that were well!
Alone you must——

EURYMACHUS
None but the conscious priest—

That too must be thy care, to chuse one faithful,
One for the purpose fit.

ÆTHON
Most worthy office! [Aside.
One to your wish, try'd in these pious secrets,
My friend of ancient date, is now in Ithaca;
Him sworn to secrecy, and well prepar'd,
I will instruct to wait you with the Queen.

EURYMACHUS
Then be propitious, Love!

ÆTHON
And thou, Revenge,
Shoot all thy fires, and wake my slumb'ring rage,
Let my past wrongs, let indignation raise
My age to emulate my youthful praise;
Let the stern purpose of my heart succeed,
Let riot, lust, and proud injustice bleed:
Grant me but this, ye gods, who favour right,
I ask no other bliss nor fond delight,
Nor envy thee, Oh, king, thy bridal night.

[Exeunt.

ACT III

Enter **ÆTHON**, **MENTOR**, and **EUMÆUS**.

ÆTHON
If virtue be abandon'd, lost and gone,
No matter for the means that wrought the ruin;
Whether the pomp of pleasure danc'd before her,
Alluring to the sense, or dreadful danger
Came arm'd with all its terrors to the onset,
She should have held the battle to the last,
Undaunted, yieldless, firm, and dy'd or conquer'd.

MENTOR
Think on what hard, on what unequal terms
Virtue, betray'd within by woman's weakness,
Beset without with mighty fears and flatteries,
Maintains the doubtful conflict—Sure if any
Have kept the holy marriage-bed inviolate,
If all our Grecian wives are not like Helen,

That praise the Queen, my royal mistress, merits.

EUMÆUS
And, Oh, impute not one unheeded word,
Forc'd from her in the bitterest pangs of sorrow,
When fierce conflicting passions strove within,
Like all the winds at once let loose upon the main,
When wild distraction rul'd—Oh, urge not that,
A blemish on her fair, her matchless fame.

ÆTHON
Oh, Mentor, and Eumæus, faithful pair!
To whom my life, my honour, all I trust,
These eyes beheld yet yielding—Cursed object!
Beheld her in the Samian king's embrace;
The sight of hell, of baleful Acheron
That rolls his livid waves around the damn'd,
Roaring and yelling on the farther shore,
Was not so terrible, so irksome to me,
As when I saw his arms infold Penelope.
I heard the fatal compact for to-night,
The joys which he propos'd, nor she deny'd—
But see she comes—

MENTOR
How much unlike a bride!

[Enter the **QUEEN**.

Behold her tears, see comfortless affliction,
Anguish, and helpless, desolate misfortune
Writ in her face.

ÆTHON
Retire; I would observe her.

[**MENTOR** and **EUMÆUS** retire to the back part of the stage.

And see! the shade of my much injured Lord starts up to blast me!

QUEEN
And dost thou only weep? Shall that put off
Th' approaching hour of shame, or save thy son?
Thou weep'st, and yet the setting sun descends
Swift to the western waves; and guilty night,
Hasty to spread her horrors o'er the world,
Rides on the dusky air—And now it comes,
The fatal moment comes, ev'n that dread time

When witches meet to gather herbs on graves,
When discontented ghosts forsake their tombs,
And ghastly roam about, and doleful groan;
And hark! the screech-owl screams, and beats the window,
With deadly wings—And hark!—More dreadful yet,
Like Thracian Tereus to unhappy Philomel,
The furious bridegroom comes,—the tyrant ravisher!
And see! the shade of my much-injur'd Lord
Starts up to blast me!—Hence!—Begone, you horrors,
For I will hide me in the arms of death,
And think on you no more—That traitor here!

[Seeing ÆTHON.

ÆTHON
Hail, beauteous Queen! The god of love salutes thee,
And thus by great Eurymachus he speaks:
Be sorrow and misfortune on thy foes;
But let thy days be crown'd with smiling peace,
Content and everlasting joy dwell with thee.

QUEEN
Com'st thou to greet me with the sounds of joy,
Thou messenger of fate?—So the hoarse raven
Croaks o'er the mansion of the dying man,
And often warns him with this dismal note,
To think upon his tomb.

ÆTHON
Or I mistook,
Or I was bid to treat of gentler matters,
Kindly to ask at what auspicious hour,
Your royal bridegroom and the priest should wait you.

QUEEN
Too well my boding heart foretold thy tidings.
Now what reply?—There is no room for choice,
'Tis one degree of infamy to doubt:
What must be must be—Let me then resolve,
'Tis only thus—no more—and I am free. [Aside.
Say to the Samian king, thy master, thus;
When Menelaus and the fate of Greece
Summon'd my Lord to Troy, he left behind him
None worthy of his place in love or empire.

ÆTHON [Aside]
How, lady!—Whither points her meaning now?

QUEEN
Say too, I've held his merit in the balance,
But find the price of honour so much greater,
That 'twere an ideot's bargain to exchange them;
Yet tell him too, I have my sex's weakness,
I have a mother's fondness in my eyes,
And all her tender passions in my heart.

ÆTHON [Aside]
Ay, there! 'tis there she's lost!

QUEEN
Nor can I bear
To see what more, far more than life I joy in,
My only pledge of love, my Lord's dear image,
My son by bloody hands mangled and murder'd;
(Oh, terrible to nature!) Therefore one,
One remedy alone is left to save me,
To shield me from a sight of so much horror,
And tell Eurymachus, I find it—here.

[She offers to stab herself; **ÆTHON** catches hold of her arm, and prevents her.

ÆTHON
Forbid it, gods! Perish the tyrant rather,
Let Samos be no more.

QUEEN
Off! Off, thou traitor!
Give way to my just rage!—Oh, tardy hand!
To what hast thou betray'd me! Let me go,
Oh, let me, let me die, or I will curse thee,
'Till hell shall tremble at my imprecations,
'Till Heav'n shall blast thee—lost!—undone for ever!

ÆTHON
Oh, trifler that I am! Mentor, Eumæus,

[They come forward.

Come to my aid!—Be calm but for a moment,
And wait to see what wonders it will shew thee.
Guard her upon your lives, remember that,
Guard her from ev'ry instrument of death,
Sooth and assuage her grief, till my return;
Unfold the mighty secret of her fate,
And once more reconcile her soul to peace.

[Exit ÆTHON.

QUEEN
And are you too my foes? Have you conspir'd
And join'd with that false Æthon to betray me?
Here sit thee down then, humbly in the dust,
Here sit, a poor, forlorn, abandon'd woman;
Cast not thy eyes up to yon' azure firmament,
Nor hope relief from thence, the gods are pitiless,
Or busy in their heav'n, and thou not worth their care;
And, Oh! Oh! cast them not on earth, to seek
For succour from the faithless race of man;
But as thou art forsaken and alone,
Hope not for help, where there is none to help thee,
But think—'tis desolation all about thee.

MENTOR
Far be that thought, to think you are forsaken;
Gods and good men shall make you still their care.
And, Oh! far be it from your faithful servants,
For all those honours mad ambition toils for,
For all the wealth that bribes the world to wickedness,
For hopes or fears, for pleasures or for pains,
To leave our royal mistress in distress.

EUMÆUS
At length time's fulness comes; and that great period,
For which so many tedious years roll'd round;
At length the white, the smiling minute comes,
To wipe the tears from those fair eyes for ever;
That good we daily pray'd for, but pray'd hopeless,
That good, which ev'n the prescience of the gods
(So doubtfully was it set down in fate,)
Uncertainly foresaw, and darkly promis'd,
That good, one day, the happiest of our lives,
Freely and fortunately brings to pass.

MENTOR
And hark! vindictive Jove prepares his thunder.

[Thunders.

Let the wrong-doer and the tyrant tremble;
The gods are present with us—And behold!
The solid gloom of night is rent asunder,
While floods of dazzling, pure ætherial light,
Break in upon the shades—She comes, she comes!
Pallas, the fautress of my master's arms.

And see where terrible in arms, majestic,
Celestial, and ineffably effulgent,
She shakes her dreadful Ægis from the clouds!
Bend, bend to earth, and own the present deity.

[It thunders again.

[The SCENE opens above, and discovers **PALLAS** in the Clouds.

[They kneel.

EUMÆUS
Daughter of mighty Jove, Tritonian Pallas,
Be favourable! Oh!—Oh! be propitious,
And save the sinking house of thy Ulysses.

MENTOR
Goddess of arts and arms, thou blue-ey'd maid,
Be favourable! Oh!—Oh! be propitious,
And glad thy suppliants with some chearful omen.

QUEEN
Virgin, begot and born of Jove alone,
Chaste, wise, victorious, if by thy assistance
The Greeks were well aveng'd on perjur'd Troy,
If by thy aid, my Lord from Thracian Rhesus
Obtain'd his snowy steeds, and brought successful
Thy fatal image to the tents of Greece;
Once more be favourable—be propitious,
Restore my Lord—Or, if that be deny'd,
Grant me to share his fate, and die with honour.

[Thunder again—The Scene closes above—They rise.

MENTOR
The goddess smiles—Most happy be the omen!
And to the left auspicious rolls the thunder.

[Enter **ÆTHON**, or Ulysses, without his disguise, magnificently arm'd and habited.

QUEEN
What other god art thou?—Oh, sacred form!
I dream, I rave!—Why put'st thou on this semblance?
What shall I call thee?—Say, speak, answer me.

[She advances two or three steps looking amazedly.

Son of Laertes! King! My Lord!—Ulysses!

ULYSSES

Why dost thou gaze?—Am I so dreadful still?
Is there so much of Æthon still about me?
Or hast thou—is it possible—forgot me?
Does not thy heart acknowledge something here?

QUEEN

Nay, 'tis, 'tis most impossible to reason.
But what have I to do with thought or reason?
Thus mad, distracted, raging with my joy,
I'll rush upon thee, clasp thee to my bosom,
And if it be delusion, let me die,
Here let me sink to everlasting rest,
Just here, and never never think again.

ULYSSES

No, live, thou great example of thy sex,
Live for the world, for me, and for thyself;
Unnumber'd blessings, honours, years of happiness,
Crowns from the gods, enrich'd with brightest stars,
All heav'n and earth united in applause,
Wait, with officious duty, to reward thee.
Live to enjoy ev'n all thou hast deserv'd,
That fulness of delight, of which these arms
And this transporting moment gives thee earnest.

QUEEN

I gaze upon thy face, and see thee here.
The sullen pow'rs below, who rule the dead,
Have listen'd to my weeping, and relented,
Have sent thee from Elysium back to me;
Or from the deep, from sea-green Neptune's seats,
Thou'rt risen like the day-star; or from heav'n
Some god has brought thee on the wings of winds;
Oh, ecstasy!—But all that I can know,
Is that I wake and live, and thou art here.

ULYSSES

Troy, I forgive thee now! Ye toils and perils
Of my past life, well are you paid at once.
For this the faithless Syrens sung in vain;
For this I 'scap'd the den of monstrous Polypheme,
Fled from Calypso's bonds and Circe's charms;
For this, seven days, and seven long winter nights,
Shipwreck'd I floated on a driving mast;
Tost by the surge, pierc'd by the bitter blasts
Of bleak north-winds, and drench'd in the chill wave,

I strove with all the terrors of the deep.

QUEEN
Yes, Thou hast borne it all, I know thou hast,
These wars, winds, magic, monsters, all for me.
Blest be the gracious gods that gave thee to me!
Say then! Oh, how shall I reward thy labours?
But I will sit and listen to thy story,
While thou recount'st it o'er; and when thou speak'st
Of difficulties hard and near to death,
I'll pity thee, and answer with my tears;
But when thou com'st to say how the gods sav'd thee,
And how thy virtue struggled through the danger,
For joy, I'll fold thee thus with soft endearments,
And crown thy conquest with ten thousand kisses.

ULYSSES
It is a heavy and a rueful tale,
But thou wilt kindly share with me in all things;
It shall be told thee then, whate'er I suffer'd,
Since, in a luckless hour, I first set out,
Ev'n to that time, when scarce twice ten days past,
As from Phæacia homeward bound to Ithaca,
A storm o'ertook and wreck'd me on the coast;
Alone and naked was I cast a-shore.
And only to these faithful two made known,
'Till Jove should point me out some opportunity,
Once more to seize my right in thee and empire.

MENTOR
'Tis hard, injurious, an offence to virtue,
To interrupt your joys, ye royal pair;
But, Oh, forgive your faithful servant's caution,
Think where you are, what eyes malicious chance
May bring to pry into the happy secret,
Untimely to disclose the fatal birth,
And rashly bring it immature to light.

ULYSSES
Mentor, thou warn'st us well—Retire, my love.

QUEEN
What must we part already?

ULYSSES
For a moment,
Like waves divided by the gliding bark,
That meet again, and mingle as before.

QUEEN
Be sure it be not longer.

ULYSSES
Sweet, it sha' not.
I'll meet thee soon, and bring our mutual blessing,
Our son, t' increase the joy.

QUEEN
I must obey you.
Remember well how long thou hast been absent,
And what a poor amends this short enjoyment makes me.
Oh, I shall die with strong desire to thee,
Shall think this one impatient minute more,
Than all thy long, long twenty years before.

[Exit.

[Enter at the other door **TELEMACHUS**.

TELEMACHUS
The Queen my mother, past she not this way?

MENTOR
She did, my Lord, ev'n now.

TELEMACHUS
Saw you not too
The Samian princess, fair Semanthe, with her?
Say, went they not together?

ULYSSES
Might I speak,
I think it is not fit they were together;
For wherefore should the queen of Ithaca
Hold commerce with the daughter of Eurymachus?
Pardon me, Sir, I fear you are offended,
And think this boldness does not fit a stranger.

TELEMACHUS
'Tis true, thou art a stranger to my eyes;
And yet, methought, thou spok'st with Æthon's voice,
Save, that th' untoward purpose of thy words
Seem'd harsh, ungentle, and not like my friend.

ULYSSES
Whate'er I seem, believe me, princely youth,

Thou hast not one, one dear selected mate,
That ought to stand before me in thy heart;
Though from your tender infancy till now,
He dwelt within thy bosom, thou in his,
Though every year has knit the band more close,
Though variance never knew you, but complying
Each ever yielded to the other's wishes,
Though you have toil'd and rested, laugh'd and mourn'd,
And ran through every part of life together,
Though he was all thy joy, and thou all his,
Yet sure he never lov'd thee more than I do.

TELEMACHUS
Whoe'er thou art (for though thou still art Æthon,
Thou art not he, but something more and greater)
I feel the force of every word thou speak'st,
My soul is aw'd with reverential fear,
A fear not irksome, for 'tis mix'd with love,
Ev'n such a fear as that we worship Heav'n with;
Oh, pardon if I err, for if thou art not
Æthon, my father's friend, thou art some god.

ULYSSES
If barely to have been thy father's friend
Could move thee to such tender, just regards,
Thus, let me thus indulge thy filial virtue,

[Embracing him.

Thus press thee in my arms, my pious son,
And while my swelling heart runs o'er with joy,
Thus tell thee that I am, I am thy father.

TELEMACHUS
Oh, most amazing!—

MENTOR
Yes, my royal charge,
At length behold thy god-like sire, Ulysses.
Blest be my age, with all its cares and sorrows,
Since it is lengthen'd out to see this day,
To give thee back, thou dear entrusted pledge,
Thus worthy as thou art, to thy great father's arms.

TELEMACHUS
Oh, 'tis most certain so, my heart confesses him,
My blood and spirits, all the pow'rs of life,
Acknowledge here the spring from whence they came.

Then let me bow me, cast me at his feet,
There pay the humble homage of my duty,
There wet the earth before him with my tears,
The faithful witnesses of love and joy:
And when my tongue for rapture can no more,
Silent, with lifted eyes, I'll praise the gods,
Who gave me back my King, my Lord, my father.

ULYSSES

Oh, rise, thou offspring of my nuptial joys,
Son of my youth, and glory of my strength,
Rob not thy father's arms of so much treasure,
But let us meet, as Jove and Nature meant us,
Thus, like a pair of very faithful friends;
And though I made harsh mention of thy love,
(Oh, droop not at the name) by blue-ey'd Pallas
I meant it not in angry, chiding mood;
But with a tender and a fond concern,
Reminded thee of what thou ow'st to honour.

TELEMACHUS

When I forget it, may the worst afflictions,
Your scorn, your hate, and infamy o'ertake me;
Be that th' important bus'ness of my life,
Let me be task'd to hunt for it through danger,
Through all the roar of the tumultuous battle,
And dreadful din of arms; there, if I fail,
May cowards say I'm not Ulysses' son,
And the great author of our race disclaim me.

ULYSSES

Oh, nobleness innate! Oh, worth divine!
Æthereal sparks! that speak the hero's lineage,
How are you pleasing to me?—So the eagle,
That bears the thunder of our grandsire Jove,
With joy beholds his hardy youthful offspring
Forsake the nest, to try his tender pinions,
In the wide untract air; till bolder grown,
Now, like a whirlwind, on the shepherd's fold
He darts precipitate, and gripes the prey;
Or fixing on some dragon's scaly hide,
Eager of combat, and his future feast,
Bears him aloft, reluctant, and in vain
Writhing his spiry tail.

TELEMACHUS

I would be active,
Get me a name distinguish'd from the herd

Of common men, a name worthy my birth.

ULYSSES
Nor shalt thou want th' occasion; now it courts thee,
Stands ready, and demands thy courage now.
Were I indeed as other fathers are;
Did I but listen to soft Nature's voice,
I should not urge thee to this high exploit,
For though it brings thee fame, it brings thee danger.

TELEMACHUS
Now by the god of war, so much the better;
Let there be honour for your son to win,
And be the danger ne'er so rude and deadly,
No matter, 'twill enhance the prize the more,
And make it lovely in a brave man's eye;
So Hydra's and Chimera's form'd in gold,
Sit graceful underneath the nodding plume,
And terribly adorn the soldier's helm.

ULYSSES
Know then, on this important night depends
The very crisis of our fate; to-night
That sleeping vengeance of the gods shall wake,
And speak confusion to our foes in thunder:
Justice entrusts her sword to this right hand,
And I will see it faithfully employ'd.

TELEMACHUS
By virtue and by arms 'tis noble work!
I burn impatient for it—Oh, my father,
Give me my portion of the glorious labour.

ULYSSES
Once more immediate danger threats thy mother,
That to avert, must be thy pious care.
While Mentor, with Eumæus and ourself,
Back'd by a chosen band, (whom how prepar'd,
How gather'd to our aid, the pressing hour
Allows not now tell) invade yon drunkards,
Immerst in riot, careless, and defying
The gods as fables, start upon them sudden,
And send their guilty souls to howl below,
Upon the banks of Styx: while this is doing,
Dar'st thou defend thy mother?

TELEMACHUS
Oh! to death,

Against united nations would I stand
Her soldier, her defence, my single breast
Oppos'd against the rage of their whole war;
She is so good, so worthy to be fought for,
The sacred cause would make my sword successful,
And gain my youth a mighty name in arms.

ULYSSES
Then prove the peril, and enjoy the fame.
Ere the mid-hour of rolling night approach,
Remember well to plant thee at that door,
Thou know'st it opens to the Queen's apartment.
To bind thee yet more firm; for, Oh, my son!

[Drawing his sword.

With powerful opposition shalt thou strive,
Swear on my sword, by thy own filial piety,
By all our race, by Pallas and by Jove,
If any of these cursed foreign tyrants,
Those rivels of thy father's love and honour,
Shall dare to pass through that forbidden entrance,
To take his forfeit life for the intrusion.

TELEMACHUS
I swear—
And may my lot in future fame

[**TELEMACHUS** kneels and kisses the sword.

Be good or evil but as I perform it.

ULYSSES
Enough—
I do believe thee.

MENTOR
Hark! my Lord!

[A confused noise is heard within.

How loud the tempest roars! The bellowing voice
Of wild, enthusiastic, raging mirth,
With peals of clamour shakes the vaulted roof.

TELEMACHUS
Such surely is the sound of mighty armies
In battle join'd, of cities sack'd at midnight,

Of many waters, and united thunders;
My gen'rous soul takes fire, and half repines,
To think she must not share the glorious danger,
Where numbers wait you, worthy of your swords.

ULYSSES
No more, thou hast thy charge, look well to that;
For these, these riotous sons of noise and uproar,
I know their force, and know I am Ulysses.
So Jove look'd down upon the war of atoms,
And rude tumultuous chaos, when as yet
Fair nature, form, and order had not being,
But discord and confusion troubled all;
Calm and serene upon his throne he sate,
Fix'd there by the eternal law of fate,
Safe in himself, because he knew his pow'r;
And knowing what he was, he knew he was secure.

[Exeunt.

ACT IV

Enter **TELEMACHUS** and **ANTINOUS**.

ANTINOUS
The king return'd? So long conceal'd in Ithaca?
Æthon the king? What words can speak my wonder?

TELEMACHUS
Yes, my Antinous, 'tis most amazing,
'Tis all the mighty working of the gods;
Unsearchable and dark to human eyes:
But, Oh, let me conjure thee by our friendship,
Since to thy faithful breast alone I've trusted
The fatal secret, to preserve it safe,
As thou wouldst do the life of thy Telemachus.

ANTINOUS
Wrong not the truth of your devoted slave,
To think he would betray you for whole worlds.
Have you not said it, that your own dear life,
And all your royal race, depends upon it?
Far from my lips, within my breast I'll keep it;
Nor breathe it softly to myself alone,
Lest some officious murmuring wind should tell it,
And babbling echoes catch the feeble sound.

TELEMACHUS

No, thou art true, such have I ever found thee;
But haste, my friend, and summon to thy aid
What force the shortness of the time allows thee;
Then with thy swiftest diligence return,
Since as I urg'd to thee before, it may
Import the safety of my royal parents.
Some black design is by these stranger-princes
Contriv'd against the honour of the Queen.

ANTINOUS

Ere night a busy rumour ran around,
Of armed parties secretly dispos'd
Between the palace-gardens and the sea;
Bold Cleon straight, and Arcas I dispatch'd
To search the truth, that known, with haste to raise
And arm our citizens for your defence:
Ere this they have obey'd me; when I've join'd
The pow'r their diligence has drawn together,
I'll wait you here again upon the instant.

[Exit.

TELEMACHUS

Oh, love! how are thy precious sweetest minutes
Thus ever cross'd, thus vex'd with disappointments!
Now pride, now fickleness, fantastic quarrels,
And sudden coldness, give us pain by turns;
Malicious meddling chance is ever busy
To bring us fears, disquiet, and delays;
And ev'n at last, when after all our waiting,
Eager, we think to snatch the dear-bought bliss,
Ambition calls us to its sullen cares,
And honour stern, impatient of neglect,
Commands us to forget our ease and pleasures,
As if we had been made for nought but toil,
And love were not the bus'ness of our lives.

[Enter **EURYMACHUS**.

EURYMACHUS

The Prince yet here! Twice have I sought, since night,
To pass in private to the Queen's apartment,
But found him still attending at the door.
What can it mean?

TELEMACHUS

It is Semanthe's father!
Ha!—Sure the gods, in pity of our loves,
Have destin'd him to 'scape Ulysses' vengeance.

EURYMACHUS

How comes it, gentle youth when wine and mirth
Cheer ev'ry heart to-night, and banish care,
I find thee pensively alone, avoiding
The pleasures and companions of thy youth,
And, like the sighing slave of sorrow, wasting
The tedious time in melancholy thought?

TELEMACHUS

Behold the ruins of my royal house,
My father's absence, and my mother's grief,
Then tell me if I have not cause too great
To mourn, to pine away my youth in sadness?

EURYMACHUS

Our daughter once was wont to share your thoughts;
Believe me, she has reason to complain,
If you prefer your solitude to her.
While here you stay, disconsolate and musing,
Lonely she sits, the tender-hearted maid,
And kindly thinks of you, and mourns your absence.

TELEMACHUS

The constant, faithful service of my life,
My days and nights devoted all to her,
Poorly repay the fair Semanthe's goodness:
Yet they are hers, ev'n all my years are hers,
My present youth, my future age, is hers,
All but this night, which here I've sworn to pass,
Revolving many a sad and heavy thought,
And ruminating on my wretched fortunes.

EURYMACHUS

How, here!—to pass it here!

TELEMACHUS

Ev'n here, my Lord.

EURYMACHUS

Fantastic accident!—Whence could this come?
[Aside.
Well, Sir, pursue your thoughts. I have some matters
Of great and high import, which, on the instant,
I must deliver to the Queen, your mother.

TELEMACHUS

Whate'er it be, you must of force delay it
Till morning.

EURYMACHUS

How, delay it!—'Tis impossible.
But wherefore?—Say.

TELEMACHUS

The Queen is gone to rest,
Oppress'd and wasted with the toil of sorrows,
Weary as miserable painful hinds,
That labour all the day to get them food,
She seeks some ease, some interval of cares,
From the kind god of sleep, and sweet repose.
Ere she retir'd she left most strict command,
None should approach her till the morning's dawn.

EURYMACHUS

Whate'er those orders were, I have my reasons
To think myself excepted. And whoe'er
Brought you the message, thro' officious haste,
Mistook the Queen, and has inform'd you wrong.

TELEMACHUS

Not so, my Lord; for, as I honour truth,
Ev'n from herself did I receive the charge.

EURYMACHUS

Vexation and delay!—Then 'tis thy own,
Thy error, and thou heard'st not what she said.
I tell thee, Prince, 'tis at her own request,
Her bidding, that this appointed hour
I wait her here. Detain me then no more
With tedious vain replies: for I must pass.

TELEMACHUS

Were it to any but Semanthe's father,
That mistress of my reason and my passions,
Who, charming both, makes both submit alike,
Perhaps I should in rougher terms have answer'd;
But here imperious love demands respect,
Constrains my temper, to my speech gives law,
And I must only say, You cannot pass.

EURYMACHUS

Ha!—Who shall bar me?

TELEMACHUS

With the gentlest words
Which reverence and duty can invent,
I will intreat you not to do a violence,
Where nought is meant to you but worthiest honour.

EURYMACHUS

Oh, trifling, idle talker!—Know, my purpose
Is not of such a light, fantastic nature,
That I should quit it for a boy's intreaty.
More than my life or empire it imports,
All that good fortune or the gods can do for me,
Depends upon it, and I will have entrance.

TELEMACHUS

Nay, then 'tis time to speak like what I am,
And tell you, Sir, you must not, nor you sha' not.

EURYMACHUS

'Twere safer for thy rash, unthinking youth
To stand the mark of thunder, than to thwart me.
Beware, lest I forget thy mother's tears,
The merit of her soft complying sorrows,
Dreadful in fury lest I rush upon thee,
Grasp thy frail life, and break it like a bubble,
To be dissolv'd, and mix'd with common air.

TELEMACHUS

Oh, 'tis long since that I have learnt to hold
My life from none, but from the gods who gave it;
Nor mean to render it on any terms,
Unless those heav'nly donors ask it back.

EURYMACHUS

Know'st thou what 'tis to tempt a rage like mine?
But listen to me, and repent thy folly,
This night, this night, ordain'd of old for bliss,
Mark'd from the rest of the revolving year,
And set apart for happiness by fate,
The charming Queen, thy mother, is my bride.

TELEMACHUS

Confusion! Curses on the tongue that spoke it!

EURYMACHUS

To-night she yields, ev'n for thy sake she yields:
To-night the lovely miser, grown indulgent,

Reveals her stores of beauty, long reserv'd,
She bids me revel with the hidden treasure,
And pay myself for all her years of coldness.

TELEMACHUS
Perdition on the falsehood!

EURYMACHUS
Dare not then
To cross my transports longer; if thou dost,
By all the pangs of disappointed love,

[Drawing.

I'll force my way thus thro' thy heart's best blood.

TELEMACHUS
How is my piety and virtue lost,
And all the heav'nly fire extinct within me!
I hear the sacred name of her that bore me
Traduc'd, dishonour'd by a ruffian's tongue,
And I am tame!—Love, and ye softer thoughts,
I give you to the winds!—Know, King of Samos,
Thy breath, like pestilential blasts, infects
The air, and grows offensive to the gods:
If thou but whisper one word more, one accent,
Against my mother's fame, it is thy last.

EURYMACHUS
Brav'd by a boy!—a boy!—the nurse's milk
Yet moist upon his lip!—feeble in infancy,
Essaying the first rudiments of manhood,
With strength unpractis'd yet, and unconfirm'd!
Oh, shame to arms!—But I have borne too long.
Fly swift, avoid the tempest of my fury,
Or thus I'll pour it in a whirlwind on thee,
Dash thee to atoms thus, and toss thee round the world.

TELEMACHUS
I laugh at all that rage, and thus I meet it.

[They fight.

EURYMACHUS
Hell and confusion!—To thy heart.

TELEMACHUS
To thine

This greeting I return.

EURYMACHUS
The Furies seize thee!

[**EURYMACHUS** falls.

Thou hast struck me to the earth, blasted my hopes;
The partial gods are leagu'd with thee against me,
To load me with dishonour—Oh, my fortune!
Where is my name in arms, the boasted trophies
Of my past life? For ever lost, defac'd,
And ravish'd from me, by a beardless stripling.

TELEMACHUS
What means this soft relenting in my soul?
What voice is this, that sadly whispers to me,
Behold, Semanthe's father bleeds to death?
Why would you urge me? [To **EURYMACHUS**.

EURYMACHUS
Off, and come not near me;
But let me curse my fate, and die contented.

TELEMACHUS
And see, he sinks yet paler to the earth,
The purple torrent gushes out impetuous,
And with a guilty deluge stains the ground.
No help at hand! What, hoa! Antinous!

[Exit.

EURYMACHUS
Let there be none, no witness of my shame,
Nor let officious art presume to offer
Its aid; for I have liv'd too long already.

[Enter **SEMANTHE**.

SEMANTHE
Sure I have staid too long; and while I sat,
Sadly attentive to the weeping Queen,
Hearing her tell of sorrows upon sorrows,
Ev'n to a lamentable length of woe,
Th' appointed hour of love pass'd by unheeded.
My lord, perhaps, will chide; Oh, no! he's gentle,
And will not urge me with my first offence.
Just as I enter'd here, the bird of night,

Ill-boding, shriek'd, and straight, methought, I heard
A low complaining voice, that seem'd to murmur
At some hard fate, and groan to be reliev'd.
Ye gracious gods, be good to my Telemachus!

EURYMACHUS
Ha! what art thou, that dost thy hostile orisons
Offer to Heaven for my mortal foe?

SEMANTHE
Guardians of innocence! ye holy pow'rs,
Defend me, save me!

EURYMACHUS
Art thou not Semanthe?

SEMANTHE
My father!—On the ground!—Bloody and pale!

[Running to him, and kneeling by him.

Oh, horror, horror!—Speak to me—Say, who—
What cursed hand has done this dreadful deed,
That with my cries I may call out for justice,
Call to the gods, and to my dear Telemachus,
For justice on my royal father's murderer!

EURYMACHUS
If there be yet one god will listen to thee,
Solicit him, that only equal power,
To rain down plagues, and fire, and swift destruction,
Ev'n all his whole artillery of vengeance,
On him, who, aided by my adverse stars,
Robb'd me of glory, love, and life—Telemachus.

SEMANTHE
What says my father?—No—it is impossible!
He could not, would not—for Semanthe's sake.

[Enter **TELEMACHUS**.

TELEMACHUS
Alas! there is none near; no help—Semanthe!

[Crying out.

EURYMACHUS
And see, he bears the trophy of his conquest;

Behold his sword yet reeking with my blood;
Then doubt no more, nor ask whom thou shouldst curse;
It is Telemachus; on whom revenge me,
But on Telemachus?—Why do I leave thee
A helpless orphan in a foreign land,
But for Telemachus?—Who tears thee from me?
Telemachus. Why is thy king and father
Stretch'd on the earth a cold and lifeless corse,
Inglorious and forgotten?—Oh, Telemachus!

[Dies.

SEMANTHE
Cruel!—unkind and cruel!—

[She faints, and falls upon the body of **EURYMACHUS**.

TELEMACHUS
She faints!
Her cheeks are cold, and the last leaden sleep
Hangs heavy on her lids—Wake, wake, Semanthe!
Oh, let me raise thee from this seat of death!

[Raising her up, and supporting her in his arms.

Lift up thy eyes. Wilt thou not speak to me?

SEMANTHE
Let me forget the use of ev'ry sense,
Let me not see, nor hear, nor speak again,
After that sight, and those most dreadful sounds.
Where am I now? What, lodg'd within thy arms!
Stand off, and let me fly from thee for ever,
Swifter than lightning, winds, or winged time;
Fly from thee till there be whole worlds to part us,
Till Nature fix her barriers to divide us,
Her frozen regions, and her burning zones,
Till danger, death and hell do stand betwixt us,
And make it fate that we shall never meet.

TELEMACHUS
'Tis just, I own thy rage is just, Semanthe;
Each fatal circumstance is strong against me.
Then if thy heart severely is resolv'd
Never to listen when I plead for mercy,
Tho' piety and honour join with love,
And humbly at thy feet make intercession,
If thou art deaf to all, then this alone

Is left me, to receive my doom, and die.

SEMANTHE
Are love, are piety, and honour, parricides?
Are they like thee? Do they delight in blood?
Oh, no! celestial sweetness dwells with them,
Friendly forgiveness, gentleness and peace,
Mercy and joy; but thou hast violated
The sacred train, brought murder in amongst them;
And see, displeas'd, to heav'n they take their flight,
And have abandon'd thee and me for ever.

TELEMACHUS
If sudden fury have not chang'd thee quite,
If there be any of Semanthe left,
One tender thought of that dear maid remaining,
Yet, I conjure thee, hear me.

SEMANTHE
'Tis in vain;
And that known voice can never charm me more.

TELEMACHUS
Be witness for me, Heav'n, with what reluctance
My hand was lifted for this fatal stroke.
With injuries which manhood could not brook,
With violence, with proud insulting scorn,
And ignominious threat'nings, was I urg'd;
Long, long I strove with rising indignation,
And long repress'd my swelling, youthful rage;
I groan'd, and felt an agony within:
'Twas hard indeed; but to myself I said,
It is Semanthe's father, and I'd bear it.

SEMANTHE
And couldst thou do no more? Call'st thou these sufferings?
These short, tumultuous, momentary passions?
What would not I have borne for thee, thou cruel one?
For thee, so fondly was my heart set on thee,
Forgetful of my tender, helpless sex,
I would have wander'd over the wide world,
Known all calamities and all distresses,
Sickness and hunger, cold and bitter want;
For thee retir'd within some gloomy cave,
I would have wasted all my days in weeping,
And liv'd and dy'd a wretch, to make thee happy;
Till I had been a story to posterity,
Till maids, in after-times, had said, behold

How much she suffer'd for the man she lov'd.

TELEMACHUS
And is there any one, the most afflicting
Of all those miseries mankind is born to,
Which for thy sake I would refuse?—But, Oh,
Mine was a harder, a severer task!
The Queen, my mother, trusted to my charge,
My royal father's honour, and my own,
The pledges of eternal fame, or infamy,
United urg'd, and call'd upon my sword.

SEMANTHE
What is this vain, fantastic pageant, honour,
This busy, angry thing, that scatters discord
Amongst the mighty princes of the earth,
And sets the madding nations in an uproar?
But let it be the worship of the great;
Well hast thou warn'd me, and I'll make it mine:
Yes, Prince, its dread command shall be obey'd;
Our Samian arms shall pour destruction on you,
Your yellow harvests and your towns shall blaze,
The sword shall rage, and universal wailings
Be heard amongst the mothers of your Ithaca,
Till war itself grow weary, and relent,
And that poor bleeding King be well reveng'd.

TELEMACHUS
Haste then, and let the trumpet sound to arms,
Semanthe's vengeance shall not be delay'd;
Prepare for slaughter and wide-wasting ruin,
Prepare to feel her wrath, ye wretched Ithacans!
Lift not a sword, nor bend a bow against her,
But all, like me, with low submission meet her,
And let us yield up our devoted lives,
Nor once implore her mercy; for, alas!
Cruel Semanthe has forgot to pardon:
For blood, destruction, and revenge she calls,
And gentleness and love are strangers to her.

SEMANTHE
Love! didst thou speak of love?—Oh, ill-tim'd thought!
Behold it there! behold the love thou bear'st me!

[Pointing to the body of **EURYMACHUS**.

Behold that, that!—more dreadful than Medusa;
It drives my soul back to her inmost fears,

And freezes ev'ry stiff'ning limb to marble.
Seest thou that gaping wound, and that black blood
Congealing on that pale, that ashy breast?
Then mark the face—how pain and rage, with all
The agonies of death, sit fresh upon it.
This was my father—
Was there none on earth,
No hand but thine?—

TELEMACHUS
Within my own sad heart
I felt the steel, before it reach'd to his.
How much more happy is his lot? The sleep
Of death is on him, and he is in peace;
While I, condemn'd to live, must mourn for him,
Mourn for myself, and, to compleat my woes,
Feel all thy pains redoubled on Telemachus.

SEMANTHE
I know thou hat'st me, and that deadly blow
Was meant to do a murder on Semanthe.
But, Oh, it needed not! for thy unkindness
Had been as fatal to me as thy sword.
If one cold look, one angry word, had told me
That thou wert chang'd, and I was grown a burthen to thee,
I should have understood thy cruel purpose,
Sat down to weep, and broke my heart, and dy'd.

TELEMACHUS
It is too much, and I will bear no more.
Oh, thou unjust, thou lovely false accuser!
How hast thou wrong'd my tender, faithful love!
In spite of all these horrors of my guilt,
And that malignant fate that doom'd me to it,
In spite of all, I will appeal to thee,
Ev'n to thyself, inhuman as thou art,
If ever maid was yet belov'd before thee,
With such heart-aching, eager, anxious fondness,
As that with which my soul desires my dear Semanthe?

SEMANTHE
Detested be the name of love for ever!
Henceforth let easy maids be warn'd by me,
No more to trust your breasts that heave with sighing,
Your moving accents, and your melting eyes;
Whene'er you boast your truth, then let them fly you,
Then scorn you, for 'tis then you mean deceiving:
If yet there should some fond believer be,

Let the false man betray the wretch, like thee,
Like thee, the lost, repenting fool disclaim,
For crowns, ambition, and your idol, fame;
When warm, when languishing with sweet delight,
Wishing she meets him, may he blast her sight
With such a murder, on her bridal night.

[Exit.

TELEMACHUS
Now arm thee for the conflict, Oh, my soul!
And see how thou canst bear Semanthe's loss;
For she is lost—most certain—gone irrevocable.
Mentor nor Æthon now, my king, my father,
Shall need t' upbraid me with th' unhappy passion—
Ha! that has wak'd a thought—'Tis certain so;
And this is all the work of cruel policy.
The danger of the Queen was from Eurymachus,
Therefore my sword was chosen to oppose it,
That it might cut the bands of love asunder.
Oh, dreamer that I was!

[Enter **ANTINOUS**, **CLEON**, and **ARCAS** with **SOLDIERS**.

ANTINOUS
My Lord, where are you?
Thus to his son, our King, the great Ulysses,
By me commands: Your royal mother's danger
Is now no more, since all the rival princes
Are in the hall beset, and ev'n this moment
Revenge and slaughter are let loose among them:
Haste then to join your godlike father's arms,
To bring your pious valour to his aid,
And share the conquest and the glory with him.

TELEMACHUS
Ha! com'st thou from the hall, Antinous?

ANTINOUS
Ev'n now, my Lord. As I was hasting hither,
It was my chance to meet my royal master;
Eager with joy, I threw me at his feet,
With wond'rous grace he rais'd me and embrac'd me,
Then bid me fly to bear his orders to you.
By the loud cries, the shouts, and clash of arms,
Which, just as I had left him, struck my ear,
I guess ere this the combat is begun.

TELEMACHUS
Yes, yes, my friend, that danger of the Queen
Is now no more. However, be thou near,
To guard her, to support her, lest the terrors
Of this tumultuous, this most dreadful night,
May shake her soul. I will obey the King,
And gladly lose the life he gave me, for him.
And since the pleasure of my days is lost,
Since my youth's dearest, only hopes are cross'd,
Careless of all, I'll rush into the war,
Provoke the lifted sword, and pointed spear,
Till, all o'er wounds, I sink amidst the slain,
And bless the friendly hand that rids me of my pain.

[Exit **TELEMACHUS**.

CLEON
Behold, my Lord, and wonder here with us;
The Samian King—

ANTINOUS
Eurymachus!—'Tis he.
Surprising accident!—Whence came this blow?
But 'tis no matter, since it makes for us,
Nor have we time to waste in vain enquiry;
Let it suffice that we have lost an enemy.
Haste to the Queen, my Cleon, and persuade her
To seek her safety with us in the city:
If she refuse, bear her away by force.
[To the **SOLDIERS**]
Do you attend him.

ARCAS
Had you ta'en my counsel,
The Prince should not have 'scap'd us.

ANTINOUS
Arcas, no!
A life like his is but a single stake,
Unworthy the contention it might cost.
Gaining the Queen, I have whate'er I wish.
Fear of the Samians and the subtle King,
Forbade my coming with a stronger power,
Lest they had ta'en th' alarm, and turn'd upon us:
Therefore I held it safer by a wile
To work upon the youth, and send him hence,
And that way gain admittance to his mother.

ARCAS
Our Ithacans, who give the King for lost,
Shall deem this tale of his return a fable;
Or tho' they should believe it, yet will join us,
And with united arms assist our cause.
Why do we linger then?—Heard you that cry?

[Cry of **WOMEN** within.

Successful Cleon, of his prey possess'd,
Leads us the way, and hastens to the city.

ANTINOUS
Come on, and let the crafty fam'd Ulysses
Repine and rage, by happier frauds excell'd.
Let the forsaken husband vainly mourn
His tedious labours, and his late return;
In vain to Pallas and to Jove complain,
That Troy and Hector are reviv'd again.
Possess'd, like happy Paris, of the fair,
I'll lengthen out my joys with ten years war,
And think the rest of life beneath a lover's care.

[Exeunt.

ACT V

SCENE, the City

Enter severally **MENTOR** and **EUMÆUS**.

EUMÆUS
Where is the joy, the boast of conquest now?
In vain we triumph o'er our foreign tyrants,
So soon to perish by domestic foes.
Why shone the great Ulysses dreadful, fierce
As Mars, and mighty as Phlegræan Jove?
Why reeks yon marble pavement with the slaughter
Of rival kings, that fell beneath his sword,
Victims to injur'd honour and revenge,
Since, by the fatal error of Telemachus,
The prize for which we fought, the Queen, is lost,
Is yielded up a prey to false Antinous?

MENTOR
He trusted in the holy name of friendship,

And, conscious of his own uprightness, thought
The man whom he had plac'd so near his heart
Had shar'd as well his virtues as his love.

EUMÆUS
How bears the Prince this chance?

MENTOR
Alas, Eumæus!
His griefs have rent my aged heart asunder.
Stretch'd on the damp unwholsome earth he lies,
Nor had my pray'rs or tears the power to raise him;
Now motionless as death his eyes are fix'd,
And then anon he starts and casts them upwards,
And groaning, cries, I am th' accurs'd of Heav'n.
My mother! my Semanthe, and my mother!

EUMÆUS
The King, whose equal temper, like the gods,
Was ever calm and content to itself,
Struck with the sudden, unexpected evil,
Was mov'd to rage, and chid him from his sight.
But now returning to the father's fondness,
He bade me seek him out, speak comfort to him,
And bring him to his arms.

MENTOR
Where have you left
Our royal master?

EUMÆUS
Near the palace gate,
Attended by those few, those faithful few,
Who dare be loyal at a time like this,
When ev'n their utmost hope is but to die for him.

MENTOR
That last relief, that refuge of despair,
Is all I fear is left us—From the city,
Each moment brings the growing danger nearer;
There's not a man in Ithaca but arms;
A thousand blazing fires make bright the streets,
Huge gabbling crowds gather, and roll along,
Like roaring seas that enter at a breach;
The neighb'ring rocks, the woods, the hills, the dales,
Ring with the deaf'ning sound, while bold rebellion
With impious peals of acclamation greets
Her trait'rous chief, Antinous—Where is then

One glimpse of safety, when we hardly number
Our friends a twentieth part of this fierce multitude?

EUMÆUS
Yet more, the Samians, by whose arms assisted
We late prevail'd against the riotous wooers,
By some sinister chance have learnt the fate
Of their dead monarch, and call loud for vengeance:
With cloudy brows the sullen captains gather
In murm'ring crowds around their weeping princess,
As if they waited from her mournful lips
The signal for destruction; from her sorrows
Catching new matter to encrease their rage,
And vowing to repay her tears, with blood.
But see, she comes, attended with her guard.

MENTOR
Retire, and let us haste to seek the Prince;
This danger threatens him. If he should meet them,
His piety would be repaid with death,
Nor could his youth or godlike courage save him,
Unequally oppress'd, and crush'd by numbers.

[Exeunt **MENTOR** and **EUMÆUS**.

[Enter **TWO SAMIAN CAPTAINS** and **SOLDIERS**, some bearing the body of **EURYMACHUS**; **SEMANTHE**
following with **OFFICERS** and **ATTENDANTS**.

SEMANTHE
Ye valiant Samian chiefs, ye faithful followers
Of your unhappy king, justly perform
Your pious office to his sacred relics;
Bear to your fleet his pale, his bloody corse,
Nor let his discontented ghost repine,
To think his injur'd ashes shall be mix'd
With the detested earth of cruel Ithaca.

1ST CAPTAIN
Oh, royal maid! whose tears look lovely on thee,
Whose cares the gods shall favour and reward,
Queen of our Samos now, to whom we offer
Our humble homage, to whose just command
We vow obedience, suffer not the seaman
T' unfurl his sails, or call the winds to swell them,
Till the fierce soldier have indulg'd his rage,
Till from the curled darlings of their youth,
And from the fairest of their virgin daughters,
We've chose a thousand victims for a sacrifice,

T' appease the manes of our murder'd lord.

SEMANTHE
Now, now, Semanthe, wilt thou name the murd'rer?
Wilt thou direct their vengeance where to strike? [Aside.
Oh, my sad heart!—Haste to dispose in safety
Your venerable load; and if you lov'd him,
If you remember what he once was to you,
How great, how good and gracious, yield this proof
Of early faith and duty to his daughter,
Restrain the soldiers' fury, till I name
The wretch by whom my royal father fell.
Let some attend the body to the shore,
The rest be near and wait me.

[Exeunt **SOME** with the **BODY**; the **REST** retire within the scene, and wait as at a distance.

[Enter at the other door **TELEMACHUS**.

TELEMACHUS
Why was I born? Why sent into the world,
Ordain'd for mischievous misdeeds, and fated
To be the curse of them that gave me being?
Why was this mass ta'en from the heap of matter,
Where innocent and senseless it had rested,
To be indu'd with form, and vex'd with motion?
How happy had it been for all that know me,
If barrenness had bless'd my mother's bed!
Nor had she been dishonour'd then, nor lost,
Nor curs'd the fatal hour in which she bore me:
Love had not been offended for Semanthe,
Nor had that fair-one known a father's loss.

SEMANTHE
What kind companion of Semanthe's woes
Is that, who, wand'ring in this dreadful night,
Sighs out her name with such a mournful accent?
Ha!—but thou art Telemachus—Let darkness
Still spread her gloomy mantle o'er thy visage,
And hide thee from these weeping eyes for ever.

TELEMACHUS
Yes, veil thy eyes, or turn them far from me;
For who can take delight to gaze on misery?
Fly from the moan, the cry of the afflicted,
From the complaining of a wounded spirit,
Lest my contagious griefs take hold on thee,
And ev'ry groan I utter pierce thy heart.

SEMANTHE

Oh, soft enchanting sorrows! Never was
The voice of mourning half so sweet—Oh, who
Can listen to the sound, and not be mov'd,
Nor bear a part, like me, and share in all his pain?
[Aside.

TELEMACHUS

But if perhaps thy fellow-creature's sufferings
Are grown a pleasure to thee, (for, alas!
Much art thou alter'd) then in me behold
More than enough to satisfy thy cruelty;
Behold me here the scorn, the easy prize,
Of a protesting, faithless, villain friend.
I have betray'd my mother, I betray'd her,
Ev'n I, her son, whom with so many cares
She nurs'd and fondled in her tender bosom.
Would I had dy'd before I saw this day!
I left her, I forsook her in distress,
And gave her to the mercy of a ravisher.

SEMANTHE

Yes, I have heard, with grief of mind redoubled,
The too hard fortune of the pious Queen;
For her my eyes enlarge and swell their streams,
Tho' well thou know'st what cause they had before
To lavish all their tears. I pity her,
I mourn her injur'd virtue: but for thee,
Whate'er the righteous gods have made thee suffer,
Just is the doom, and equal to thy crimes.

TELEMACHUS

'Tis justice all, and see I bow me down
With patience and submission to the blow;
Nor is it fit that such a wretch as I am
Should walk with face erect upon the earth,
And hold society with man—Oh, therefore
Let me conjure thee by those tender ties
Which held us once, when I was dear to thee,
And thou to me, as life to living creatures,
Or light and heat to universal nature,
The comfort and condition of its being,
Complete th' imperfect vengeance of the gods,
Call forth the valiant Samians to thy aid,
Bid them strike here, and here revenge—

SEMANTHE

Oh, hold!
Stay thy rash tongue, nor let it speak of horrors
That may be fatal to—

TELEMACHUS
What mean'st thou?

SEMANTHE
Something
For which I want a name—Is there none near?
No conscious ear to catch the guilty sound?
None to upbraid my weakness, call me parricide,
And charge me as consenting to the murder?
For, Oh, my shame, my shame! I must confess it,
Tho' piety and honour urg'd me on,
Tho' rage and grief had wrought me to distraction,
I durst not, could not, would not once accuse thee.

TELEMACHUS
And wherefore art thou merciful in vain?
Oh, do not load me with that burthen, life,
Unless thou give me love, to cheer my labours.
Tell me, Semanthe, is it, is it thus
The bride and bridegroom meet? Are tears and mourning,
This bitterness of grief, and these lamentings,
Are these the portion of our nuptial night?

SEMANTHE
But thou, thou only didst prevent the joy,
'Tis thou hast turn'd the blessing to a curse:
Live, therefore, live, and be, if it be possible,
As great a wretch as thou hast made Semanthe.

TELEMACHUS
It shall be so; I will be faithful to thee,
For days, for months, for years, I will be miserable,
Protract my suff'rings ev'n to hoary age,
And linger out a tedious life in pain;
In spite of sickness and a broken heart,
I will endure for ages to obey thee.

SEMANTHE
Oh, never shalt thou know sorrows like mine!
Never despair, never be curs'd as I am.
Yes, I will open my afflicted breast,
And sadly shew thee ev'ry secret pain,
Tho' hell and darkness with new monsters teem,
Tho' furies, hideous to behold, ascend,

Toss their infernal flames, and yell around me;
Tho' my offended father's angry ghost
Should rise all pale and bloody just before me,
Till my hair started up, my sight were blasted,
And ev'ry trembling fibre shook with horror;
Yet—yet—Oh, yet, I must confess I love thee!

TELEMACHUS
Then let our envious stars oppose in vain
Their baleful influence, to thwart our joys;
My love shall get the better of our fate,
Prevent the malice of that hard decree,
That seem'd to doom us to eternal sorrows;
And yet in spite of all we will be happy.

SEMANTHE
Let not that vain, that faithless hope deceive thee,
For 'tis resolv'd, 'tis certainly decreed,
Fix'd as that law by which imperial Jove,
According to his prescience and his pow'r,
Ordains the sons of men to good or evil;
'Tis certain, ev'n our love, and all the mis'ries
Which must attend that love, are not more certain,
Than that this moment we must part for ever.

TELEMACHUS
How! Part for ever? That's a way indeed
To make us miserable. Is there none,
No other sad alternative of grief,
No other choice but this?—What, must we part for ever?

SEMANTHE
Oh, sigh not, nor complain! Is not thy hand
Stain'd with my father's blood? Justice and nature,
The gods demand it, and we must obey:
Yes, I must go, the pressing minutes call me,
Where these fond eyes shall never see thee more,
No more with languishing delight gaze on thee,
Feed on thy face, and fill my heart with pleasure,
Where day and night shall follow one another,
Tedious alike and irksome, and alike
Wasted in weary loneliness and weeping.

TELEMACHUS
Here then, my soul, take thy farewel of happiness;
That and Semanthe fly together from thee:
Henceforth renounce all commerce with the world,
Nor hear, nor see, nor once regard what passes.

Let mighty kings contend, ambitious youth
Arm for the battle, seasons come and go,
Spring, summer, autumn, with their fruitful pleasures,
And winter with its silver frost, let Nature
Display in vain her various pomp before thee,
'Tis wretched all, 'tis all not worth thy care,
'Tis all a wilderness, without Semanthe.

SEMANTHE
One last, one guilty proof, how much I love thee;
(Forgive it, gods!) Ceraunus and the Samians
Shall bring thee from me, ere I part from Ithaca.
That done, I'll haste, I'll fly, as I have sworn,
For thy lov'd sake, far from the sight of man,
Fly to the pathless wilds, and sacred shades,
Where Dryads and the mountain-nymphs resort,
There beg the rural deities to pity me,
To end my woes, and let me on their hills,
Like Cyparissus, grow a mournful tree,
Or melt, like weeping Byblis, to a fountain.

TELEMACHUS
Since fate divides us then, since I must lose thee,
For pity's sake, for love's, Oh, suffer me,
Thus languishing, thus dying, to approach thee,
And sigh my last adieu upon thy bosom!
Permit me, thus, to fold thee in my arms,
To press thee to my heart, to taste thy sweets,
Thus pant, and thus grow giddy with delight.
Thus for my last of moments gaze upon thee,
Thou best, thou only joy—thou lost Semanthe!

SEMANTHE
For ever I could listen; but the gods,
The cruel gods, forbid, and thus they part us.
Remember, Oh, remember me, Telemachus!
Perhaps thou wilt forget me; but no matter;
I will be true to thee, preserve thee ever
The sad companion of this faithful breast,
While life and thought remain; and when at last
I feel the icy hand of death prevail,
My heart-strings break, and all my senses fail,
I'll fix thy image in my closing eye,
Sigh thy dear name, then lay me down and die.

[Exit.

TELEMACHUS

And whither wilt thou wander, thou forlorn,
Abandon'd wretch?—The King thy father comes;
Fly from his angry frown, no matter whither;
Seek for the darkest covert of the night,
Seek out for death, and see if that can hide thee,
If there be any refuge thou canst prove,
Safe from pursuing sorrow, shame, and anxious love.

[Exit.

[Enter **ULYSSES**, **EUMÆUS**, and **ATTENDANTS**.

ULYSSES
To doubt if there be justice with the gods,
Or if they care for aught below, were impious.
Oft have I try'd, and ever found them faithful;
In all the various perils of my life,
In battles, in the midst of flaming Troy,
In stormy seas, in those dread regions where
Swarthy Cimmerians have their dark abode,
Divided from this world, and borderers on hell,
Ev'n there the providence of Jove was with me,
Defended, cheer'd, and bore me thro' the danger:
Nor is his pow'r, nor is my virtue less,
That I should fear this rude, tumultuous herd.

EUMÆUS
So feeble is our band, so few our friends,
We hope not safety from ourselves, but thee;
In thee, our king, we trust, in thee, our hero,
Favour'd of Heav'n, in all thy wars victorious.
But see where proud rebellion comes against thee,

[Shout.

Securely fierce, and breathing bold defiance.
Now let our courage and our faith be try'd,
And if, unequal to thy great example,
We cannot conquer like thee, yet we can die for thee.

[Shout, drums, and trumpets; then enter **ANTINOUS**, **CLEON**, and **SOLDIERS**.

ANTINOUS
What bold invader of our laws and freedom,
Usurps the sacred name of king in Ithaca?
Who dares to play the tyrant in our state,
And in despite of hospitable Jove,
Defames our island with the blood of strangers?

ULYSSES
Have you forgot me then, you men of Ithaca?
Did I for this, amongst the Grecian heroes,
Go forth to battle in my country's cause?
Have I by arms and by successful counsels
Deserv'd a name from Asia's wealthy shores
Ev'n to the western ocean, to those bounds
That mark the great Alcides' utmost labours,
And am I yet a stranger here—at home?

ANTINOUS
And wherefore didst thou leave those distant nations,
Thro' which thy name and mighty deeds were spread?
We never sought to know thee, and now known,
Regard thee not, unless it be to punish
Thy violation of our public peace.

ULYSSES
And dost thou dare, dost thou, audacious slave!
Thou rash misleader of this giddy crowd,
Dost thou presume to match thyself with me,
To judge between a monarch and his people?
If Heav'n had not appointed me thy master,
Yet it had made me something more than thou art,
Then when it made me what I am—Ulysses!

ANTINOUS
Then be Ulysses! echo it again,
And see what homage these will pay the sound:

[Pointing to the **SOLDIERS**.

Tell them the story of your Trojan wars,
How Hector drove you headlong to the shore,
And threw his hostile fires amidst your fleet;
Then mark with what applause they will receive thee.
Say, countrymen, will you revenge the princes
This wanderer has slain, and join with me?

OMNES
Antinous! Antinous!

ANTINOUS
What of your monarch?

OMNES
Drive him out to banishment.

ULYSSES

Were there no gods in heav'n, or were they careless,
And Jove had long forgot to wield his thunder,
And dart destruction down on crimes like thine;
Yet, traitor, hope not thou to 'scape from justice,
Nor let rebellious numbers swell thy pride;
For know, Ulysses is alone sufficient
To punish thee, and on thy perjur'd head
Revenge the wrongs of love and injur'd majesty.

ANTINOUS

And see, I stand prepar'd to meet thy vengeance;
Exert thy kingly pow'r, and summon all
Thy useful arts and courage to thy aid:
And since thy faithful Diomede is absent,
Since valiant Ajax, with his seven-fold shield,
No more shall interpose 'twixt thee and danger,
Invoke those friendly gods, whose care thou art,
And let them save thee, now assert thy cause,
And render back to thy despairing arms
The beauteous Queen, whom, in despite of them
And thee, this happy night I made my prize.

ULYSSES

Hear this, ye gods! he triumphs in the rape.
Most glorious villain!—But we pause too long.
On then, and tempt our fate, my gallant friends,
From this defier of the gods, this monster;
Let us redeem my Queen, or die together;
And, equal to our great forefathers' fame,
Descend and join those demi-gods of Greece,
Who with their blood enrich'd the Dardan plains,
To vindicate a husband's sacred right.

[Shout.

[Enter **ARCAS** wounded.

ANTINOUS

What means that sudden thunder-clap of tumult?
Art thou not Arcas?—Thou art faint and bloody.

ARCAS

I have paid you the last office of my friendship;
Scarce have I breath enough to speak your danger:
The furious Samians, led by young Telemachus,
Resistless, fierce, and bearing all before them,

Have from the castle forc'd the captive Queen;
Fir'd with success, they drive our fainting troops,
And hither urge their way with threat'ning cries,
Loudly demanding your devoted head,
A just atonement for their murder'd lord.

ULYSSES
Celestial pow'rs! ye guardians of the just!
This wond'rous work is yours, and yours be all the praise.

ANTINOUS
Confusion!—Wherefore didst thou not proclaim
My innocence, and warn them of their error?

ARCAS
Behold these wounds, through which my parting soul
Is hasting forth, and judge my truth by them.
Whate'er I could, I urg'd in thy defence;
But all was vain: with clamorous impatience,
They broke upon my speech, and swore 'twas false;
Their Queen, the fair Semanthe, had accus'd thee,
And fix'd her royal father's death on thee.
If any way be left yet, haste and fly;
Th' inconstant, faithless Ithacans join with them,
And all is lost—What dearer pledge than life
Can friendship ask? Behold I give it for thee.

[Dies.

[Shout.

ULYSSES
They come! Success and happiness attend us!
Pallas, and my victorious son, fight for us!

ANTINOUS
Thou and thy gods at last have got the better.
[To **ULYSSES**.
Yet know, I scorn to fly; that great ambition
That bid me first aspire to love and empire,
Still brightly burns, and animates my soul.
Be true, my sword, and let me fall reveng'd,
And I'll forgive ill fortune all besides.

[**ULYSSES**, **ANTINOUS**, and their **PARTIES**, fight.

[Enter **TELEMACHUS**, **CERAUNUS**, and **SAMIAN SOLDIERS**; they join **ULYSSES**, and drive **ANTINOUS**, **CLEON**, and the rest off the stage. Then enter at one door **ULYSSES**, at the other the **QUEEN**, **MENTOR**, and **ATTENDANTS**.

ULYSSES
My Queen! my love!

[Embracing.

QUEEN
My hero! my Ulysses!
Once more thou art restor'd, once more I hold thee!
At length the gods have prov'd us to the utmost,
Are satisfy'd with what we have endur'd,
And never will afflict nor part us more.
'Tis not in words to tell thee what I've felt,
The sorrows and the fears; ev'n yet I tremble,
Ev'n yet the fierce ideas shock my soul,
And hardly yield to wonder and to joy.

MENTOR
A turn so happy, and so unexpected,
None but those over-ruling pow'rs who caus'd it
Could have foreseen. The beauteous Samian Princess,
Within whose gentle breast revenge and tenderness
Long strove, and long maintain'd a doubtful conflict,
At length was vanquish'd by prevailing love,
And, happily, to save the Prince, imputed
To false Antinous her father's death.
Heav'n has approv'd the fraud of fond affection,
The just deceit, a falshood fair as truth,
Since 'tis to that alone we owe our safety.

[Enter **TELEMACHUS**.

TELEMACHUS
Here let me kneel, and with my tears atone

[Kneeling.

The rash offences of my heedless youth;

[**ULYSSES** raises him.

Here offer the first trophies of my sword,
And once more hail my father King of Ithaca.
Antinous, the rebel faction's chief,
Is now no more, and your repenting people

Wait with united homage to receive you;
The strangers too, to whom we owe our conquest,
Haste to embark, and set their swelling sails,
To bear the sad Semanthe back to Samos.
Joy, like the cheerful morning, dawns on all,
And none but your unhappy son shall mourn.

ULYSSES
Like thee, the pangs of parting love I've known,
My heart like thine has bled——But, Oh, my son!
Sigh not, nor of the common lot complain;
Thou, that art born a man, art born to pain:
For proof, behold my tedious twenty years,
All spent in toil, and exercis'd in cares.
'Tis true, the gracious gods are kind at last,
And well reward me here for all my sorrows past.

[Exeunt.

EPILOGUE

Spoken by **SEMANTHE**

Just going to take water, at the stairs
I stopp'd, and came again to beg your pray'rs;
You see how ill my love has been repaid,
That I am like to live and die a maid;
Poetic rules and justice to maintain,
I to the woods am order'd back again,
To Madam Cynthia and her virgin train.
'Tis an uncomfortable life they lead;
Instead of quilts and down, the sylvan bed,
With skins of beasts, with leaves and moss, is spread;
No morning toilets do their chambers grace,
Where famous pearl cosmetics find a place,
With powder for the teeth, and plaister for the face.
But in defiance of complexion, they,
Like arrant housewives, rise by break of day,
Cut a brown crust, saddle their nags, and mounting,
In scorn of the green-sickness, ride a hunting.
Your sal, and hartshorn drops, they deal not in;
They have no vapours, nor no witty spleen.
No coffee to be had; and I am told,
As to the tea they drink, 'tis mostly cold.
For conversation, nothing can be worse,
'Tis all amongst themselves, and that's the curse;

One topic there, as here, does seldom fail,
We women rarely want a theme to rail;
But, bating that one pleasure of backbiting,
There is no earthly thing they can delight in.
There are no Indian houses to drop in,
And fancy stuffs, and chuse a pretty screen,
To while away an hour or so—I swear
These cups are pretty, but they're deadly dear;
And if some unexpected friend appear,
The dev'l!—Who could have thought to meet you here?
We should but very badly entertain
You that delight in toasting and champagne.
But keep your tender persons safe at home;
We know you hate hard riding: but if some
Tough, honest country fox-hunter would come,
Visit our goddess, and her maiden court,
'Tis ten to one, but we may shew him sport.

Nicholas Rowe – A Concise Bibliography

Poems
A Poem upon the Late Glorious Successes of Her Majesty's Arms (1707)
Poems on Several Occasions (1714)
Maecenas. Verses occasion'd by the honours conferr'd on the Right Honourable Earl of Halifax (1714)
Ode for the New Year MDCCXVI (1716)

Original Plays
The Ambitious Stepmother (1700)
Tamerlane (1702)
The Biter (1705)
Ulysses (1705)
The Royal Convert (1707)
The Tragedy of Jane Shore (1714)
Lady Jane Grey (1715)

Adaptations and Translations
The Fair Penitent (1702/3), an adaptation of Massinger and Field's The Fatal Dowry
Lucan (1718), a paraphrase of the Pharsalia
Callipaedia (date unknown), translation of Claude Quillet

Edited Works
The Works of William Shakespear (London: 1709), first modern edition of the plays.

Miscellaneous Works
Memoir of Boileau (date unknown), prefixed to translation of Lutrin
Some Account of the Life of Mr. William Shakespear

The Garden of Kama by Laurence Hope

The pseudonym for Adela Florence Cory Nicolson

Later published in the United States as India's Love Lyrics

Adela Florence Cory was born on 9th April 1865 at Stoke Bishop, Gloucestershire, the second of three daughters to Colonel Arthur Cory and Fanny Elizabeth Griffin. Adele was initially raised by relatives as her father was employed in Lahore in the service of the British army.

Eventually at 16, in 1881, she went to India to be reunited with her family. Her father was now the editor of the Lahore arm of The Civil and Military Gazette. Adela's sisters Annie Sophie and Isabel also has literary careers. Annie would go on to write popular, racy novels while Isabel assisted and then succeeded their father as editor of the Sind Gazette.

In April 1889 Adela married Colonel Malcolm Hassels Nicolson, a man twice her age and the commandant of the 3rd Battalion, the Baluch Regiment. Nicolson was a reputed action man and linguist and introduced his young wife to the glories of India, its customs, culture and food.

This deep immersion helped give the couple an eccentric reputation. In an expedition to the Zhob Valley in 1890 she disguised herself as a Pathan boy to follow her husband through the passes along the Afghan border. They would eventually live in Mhow for nearly a decade.

In 1901, she published 'Garden of Kama', which, a year later, was published in America with the title 'India's Love Lyrics'.

She originally attempted to pass the work off as translations of various poets, but this claim soon fell away. Still she shied away from any public recognition and used the publishing pseudonym of Laurence Hope to further shield herself.

Adela's poems were often suffused with imagery and symbols from the poets of the North-West Frontier and the Sufi poets of Persia and helped make her one of the most popular romantic poets of the Edwardian era with their themes of unrequited love, loss and often, the death that followed such an unhappy state of affairs.

Two months after Nicolson died in a prostate operation, Adela, who had been prone to depression since childhood, committed suicide by poisoning herself with perchloride of mercury.

Adela Florence Cory Nicolson died at the age of 39 on 4th October 1904 in Madras.

Index of Contents